Aural Awareness

Aural Awareness

Principles and Practice

GEORGE PRATT
with Michael Henson and Simon Cargill

OXFORD UNIVERSITY PRESS

*This book has been printed digitally and produced in a standard specification
in order to ensure its continuing availability*

OXFORD
UNIVERSITY PRESS

Great Clarendon Street, Oxford OX2 6DP

Oxford University Press is a department of the University of Oxford.
It furthers the University's objective of excellence in research, scholarship,
and education by publishing worldwide in

Oxford New York

Auckland   Cape Town Dar es Salaam Hong Kong Karachi
Kuala Lumpur Madrid Melbourne Mexico City Nairobi
New Delhi Shanghai Taipei Toronto
With offices in
Argentina Austria Brazil Chile Czech Republic France Greece
Guatemala Hungary Italy Japan South Korea Poland Portugal
Singapore Switzerland Thailand Turkey Ukraine Vietnam

Oxford is a registered trade mark of Oxford University Press
in the UK and in certain other countries
Published in the United States
by Oxford University Press Inc., New York

ISBN 0-19-879021-X

Contents

Acknowledgements

When I was appointed to the Music Department of Huddersfield University (then Polytechnic) in 1985 I was offered the help of a Research Assistant to establish the unit for Research into Applied Musical Perception (RAMP). Few institutions in Higher Education would show such faith in a new and unproven project. Appropriately to a polytechnic, the research was of a thoroughly practical kind, identifying the aural needs of musical practitioners and devising methods of satisfying those needs. The Music Department at Huddersfield was, and remains, fertile ground for the seeds of such inquiry. In the first year of the degree and diploma courses, every student composes, performs, and studies history and repertoire. It was relatively easy, therefore, to determine with their help the skills and perceptions that are needed in what are now commonly recognized as the three valid spheres of musical activity: composing, performing and listening.

The first Research Assistant to the RAMP Unit was Michael Henson. He surveyed students not only at Huddersfield but also at other places, conservatoires and universities, together with individual practising performers and composers within the musical profession. This led us quickly to the conclusion that most conventional aural training is quite inadequate, over-stressing the significance of facility in perceiving, identifying and naming aspects of pitch and duration, at great cost to other expressive musical elements which in practice are no less important. We therefore devised a course for first-year degree students which laid heavy stress on those elements. This formed the contents of the 1990 edition of this book. Michael Henson played a particularly vital role in structuring the ideas we discussed together and in inventing ways of presenting them. Many of the group and 'do-it-yourself' exercises come from his fertile mind.

His successor, Simon Cargill, before his tragically early death in 1993, had an important influence upon the final drafting. Where familiarity with the course, already taught four times, might have bred carelessness of expression or assumptions that concepts were clear, he questioned every issue afresh, and contributed quite fundamentally, especially to Chapter 8, 'Structure', and to the suggested methods of assessment in Appendix 1.

Thanks are also due to my colleague, David Lennox, who, in helping to teach the course for two years, questioned many details in the 'teaching material' provided for him, and to Professor Kate Covington of the University of Kentucky, who similarly cast a critical eye over an early draft while working in the field of aural perception on a sabbatical visit to the Music Department at Huddersfield.

Chapter 12, 'Playing from memory', benefited greatly from input by Karen Humphreys, a research student investigating the acquisition and uses of musical memory. I am also indebted to Dr John Sloboda, musical psychologist and Associate of the RAMP Unit, who gave invaluable advice and constant encouragement to the whole project from its inception in 1985.

Finally, we must all thank those cohorts of first-year music students at Huddersfield for their response to what we offered them. It was always animated, often enthusiastic, at times invaluably critical. They constantly showed us ways of extending and refining not only the content of the course we had been developing for them but also the ways in which it may be presented.

By a happy accident of timing, the National Curriculum Music Working Group was formed shortly after the first edition of this book appeared in print. As a member of that Working Group, I was able to contribute to it many of the ideas developed by the RAMP Unit. These were incorporated into our proposals for the National Curriculum in Music for England and Wales, and this revised edition of *Aural Awareness* reflects, in turn, the application of these ideas to the statutory Curriculum for 'Music 5 to 14' as well as retaining the initial undergraduate focus of the techniques and materials we had first developed.

I have been surprised and delighted at the universality of the principles involved. A child of five can discriminate between the sounds, say, of a harpsichord and a piano; a teenager may acquire the timbral memory to identify a fortepiano as different from a modern grand piano; piano students at conservatoire or university will prefer the sound of one piano to another to practise on; an experienced professional concert pianist will normally recognize, blindfolded, a familiar concert grand simply by its sound. So the principles of timbral discrimination are common to all ages and levels of aural maturity: only the degree of sophistication changes.

This revised edition of *Aural Awareness* is therefore addressed to anyone who wishes to extend either their own level of musical awareness and aural perception or that of pupils from early schooling to adulthood. I have in places added suggested tasks and aural challenges for the less experienced. Elsewhere, I have exhorted teachers and students to invent their own exercises and apply newly-found and developing aural skills to the musical repertoire of their choice.

In a further development still, the Music Department at the University of Huddersfield is devising a highly interactive Computer Assisted Learning package designed to improve musicians' aural awareness. The *Computer Assisted Learning for Musical Awareness* (CALMA) project, supported by the Higher Education Funding Council's *Fund for the Development of Teaching and Learning* initiative, is based on many of the ideas in this book. The software features exercises on all the musical elements explored in Chapter 2, and is intended to be used as a learning resource to support individual study or as a preparation for class work.

The package, whilst including traditional pitch and rhythm exercises, is designed to complement established aural training methods by also investigating elements such as timbre and texture. Using commercial recordings as sound sources, the exercises are placed in a real and satisfying musical context. In addition, the package allows users to manipulate computer-generated sounds in real time, so that they can hear immediately the results of their experimentation. The final CD-ROM package, available from the beginning of the millennium, is designed to run on both IBM-compatible PC and Apple Mac.

Acknowledgement is made to the following copyright-holders for material reproduced in the music examples.

Ex. 2.2b from *Historical Anthology of Music, Vol. II*, Harvard University Press, 1950.

Ex. 3.7a from *Threnody for the Victims of Hiroshima* by Krzysztof Penderecki, published by Deshon Music Inc and PWM Editions USA, 1960.

Exs. 4.5b and 4.5c transcribed from A. M. Jones, *Studies in African Music*, Oxford University Press, 1959.

Exs. 4.10a, 6.2a and 12.6a from *Six Metamorphoses after Ovid* (Op. 49) by Benjamin Britten, published by Boosey and Hawkes, 1952.

Ex. 9.2a from *Serenade for Tenor, Horn and Strings* (Op. 31) by Benjamin Britten, published by Boosey and Hawkes, 1943.

Ex. 9.8a from Symphony (Op. 21) by Anton Webern, published by Universal Edition, 1928.

George Pratt
Huddersfield University

Introduction

An alarmingly large proportion of musicians, questioned about their own experiences of aural training, admit that they disliked it, thought they were bad at it, and have found it largely irrelevant to their subsequent engagement in music. Something is clearly wrong. Aural perception is self-evidently indispensable in musical activity, in creating through composing, re-creating in performance, responding as a critical listener. Either many musicians should have taken up other careers, as brain-surgeons, say, or bookmakers, or else the content and methods of aural training and testing are inappropriate to their presumed purpose of developing musical perceptions.

The claim of this book is that the training is at fault rather than the musicians who undergo it. In particular its contents, the skills which are meant to be taught, are heavily influenced by whether or not they can be assessed. This is in part the result of the conflict between an educational system which demands identifiable measures of achievement and the study of an art which is often very subjective and defies precise measurement. For example, if someone plays you a 'D' on the piano and you write it down accurately by relative or perfect pitch, you can be awarded a mark for it. But no one can award you marks for perceiving the balance and tone-quality of that same 'D' at the opening of Beethoven's Second Symphony.

So, to meet the demand for assessment, much aural training is directed towards testing of what is right or wrong, and the most convenient material for this is the pitch and duration of notes. All the following, the basic diet of so many aural examinations, come into this category:

1. identifying letter-names and time-values of notes as they are played, individually or in motivic groups;
2. imitative singing and clapping of melodies and rhythms;
3. writing music down at various levels of complexity, from individual intervals, through single-line melodies, two-part counterpoint and four-part harmony, to extended pieces of piano music in idioms so idiosyncratic that no help can be sought from aural intuition;
4. naming all the pitch-based musical phenomena such as cadences, modulations and harmonic progressions;
5. spotting wrong notes in performance.

All these depend on perceiving and identifying pitches and durations.

It is significant that many of those who find positive delight in such tests, and the training that leads to them, have perfect pitch. For them, pitch identification is simply a matter of naming an aural phenomenon as clearly identifiable as are, to most people, the colours red and blue or the tastes of chocolate and Camembert.

All this is not to suggest that pitch and duration are unimportant: far from it. In most music of the western tonal tradition and of other cultures throughout the world, the accuracy of pitched notes, their relationship to one another in melody, counterpoint and harmony, and their duration in metre and rhythm are central elements of musical expression. Yet the overwhelming importance ascribed to them in most conventional aural training distorts our real musical needs. Since the first version of this book, in 1990, there have been many changes for the better. The National Curriculum in Music, taught to all state-educated children from ages 5 to 14, has at its heart a series of 'musical elements'—not only pitch and duration, but also dynamics, tempo, timbre, texture, and structure. These are common to all three 'Key Stages' of the Curriculum, though the implications of each become more sophisticated at each stage (see Table).

2

Element	Key Stage 1	Key Stage 2	Key Stage 3
Pitch	High/low	Gradation of pitch	Various scales and modes
Duration	Long/short; pulse or beat; rhythm	Groups of beats; rhythm	Syncopation; rhythm
Dynamics	Loud/quiet/silence	Different levels of volume; accent	Subtle differences in volume
Tempo	Fast/slow	Different speeds	Subtle differences in speed
Timbre	Quality of sound	Different qualities	Different ways timbre is changed; different qualities
Texture	Several sounds played or sung at the same time; one sound on its own	Different ways sounds are put together	Density and transparency of instrumentation; polyphony; harmony
The use of the above within structure	Different sections; repetition	Different ways sounds are organized in simple forms	Forms based on single ideas; forms based on alternating ideas; forms based on developmental ideas

In a complementary spirit, the Aural Tests of the Associated Board of the Royal Schools of Music (ABRSM) have been significantly revised, and now include questions at all Grades requiring a level of judgement rather than solely a memory for pitches, durations, and musical terminology.

Nevertheless, we still neglect, to a greater or lesser degree, all of the following:

1. the range and tessitura of instruments and voices;
2. the density and the distribution of sounds and the textures within which they are performed;
3. the range of timbral colours, of dynamics, articulations and phrasing of which they are capable;
4. where sounds are positioned in space and how they relate to each other structurally;
5. above all, the variations in pace at which all these elements may occur.

Nor does the damage end in simple neglect. It influences attitudes and opinions too. Narrow training programmes, far from increasing aural awareness, may actually close ears and minds.

3

Introduction

We are taught to focus so nearly exclusively on the pitches and rhythms of tonal tunes that many committed musicians find it difficult to identify points of contact with contemporary western music, or with the riches of other musical cultures lacking such tunes. To many, the implied indoctrination that music consists of tonal tunes and modal melodies carries with it the corollary that, if these are missing, it cannot be proper music.

Clearing the ground

The purpose of this book is to redress the balance, to focus attention sharply on the neglected elements of musical expression. A first step in doing so will be to take the perception of pitch and duration through dictations out of limited classroom time. Younger musicians will need more direct personal input by teachers to develop accuracy of pitch and rhythmic perception and notation, in their performing, composing, and listening and appraising. But such skills can be developed, at least in degree, diploma, and sixth-form courses, without eating into the precious weekly hour, perhaps more, perhaps less, allocated to aural training. The place to do so is in the music library or at home, with gramophones, CD players or personal stereos feeding material to you through headphones. Although some guidance is valuable, perhaps in the form of a 'work sheet' prepared by a tutor, students can actually find material for themselves. The first eight bars of a minuet from almost any Haydn string quartet, for example, is preferable to the eight-bar melody of studied anonymity, written by last year's Board of Examiners and played on the piano by a bored teacher. The music is by a composer of stature; it is played by distinguished performers on first-rate instruments; you can take down a first violin melody or a rhythm or a progression of harmonies, adding if you wish the audible phrasing, articulation and dynamics. The available repertoire is virtually limitless; the musical advantages are enormous.

So too are the methodological advantages. If eight bars are too taxing, take four, or two. If the conventional four or five hearings are too few, treat yourself to more. The task can be tailored

4

exactly to your own capabilities. You are sure of *some* measure of success, while you are spared the embarrassment of public failure: it is a well-known phenomenon that other people are always better at 'aural' than you!

The CD player is a particularly convenient device to use for repeated playings of a musical fragment as it allows very exact cueing. Cassette tape players with counters are nearly as accurate. If you still depend on a library of LP records you tend to be limited to beginnings—of works or of movements—since you need to begin and end the music you feed to yourself at exactly the same points each time, starting from the opening of a side or a band. You could overcome this problem, of course, by recording your chosen bars on tape and cueing with a tape counter.

The only other requirement is a score, from which to take any prerequisite information such as the key within which you will be writing down from dictation. The score, of course, also provides the unequivocal 'right answer'.

But before embracing too enthusiastically this 'do-it-yourself' approach to the pitch and rhythm elements which monopolize so much of traditional aural training programmes and the assessable tests towards which they lead, it is still worth considering how important these skills are to practising musicians. Writing music down accurately as it is 'dictated' by your imagination, in your head, is still useful to a composer and an arranger; but we may find ourselves increasingly storing composition in digital recording rather than in notation on paper. That in turn can increasingly be printed out by computerized 'desk-top publishing' systems. 'Midi' links between instrument and computer now provide a direct print-out in staff notation of what you have just played, and the development of this technique is continuing at an amazing pace. It is to some degree useful for a performer to be able to communicate clearly in words and so to know that a particular interval is called a minor sixth or that a cadence is 'perfect' or 'interrupted'; but the neglected elements listed above are generally far more significant. As for listeners, the greater need is to hear what a musical phenomenon *is* rather than to know what it is *called*.

How to use this book

However much importance you attach to acquiring skills in perceiving, identifying and writing down pitches and durations in their various musical functions, that training can now go on out of the classroom. The ground is cleared, and the seeds of other musical ideas, contained in the following chapters, can be sown. As you read on through the book, various alternative strategies are open to you. One is to work consistently through, from beginning to end. For anyone or any group of students at undergraduate level, this is probably the best approach. Sixth-form students, too, can work in this way, though the pace may need to be a little steadier. Less experienced students will need the help of a teacher to identify aural challenges and to devise exercises which will develop and extend aural skills. Merely listening to 'Tallis' Canon' (Chapter 2.2a) will not be the best introduction to 'Metre' for a primary school class. But marching in step to the piece—or any other in 4-time—will help to internalize a sense of pulse in a regular recurring pattern (and indeed, the National Curriculum requires it in Key Stage 1). Then try marching in 3-time—soldiers with a limp!

Private music teachers will find here many ideas to stimulate and develop awareness in their instrumental or singing pupils. The 'Aural Tests' of such international examination boards as the Associated Board of the Royal Schools of Music and Trinity College London resonate clearly with the approaches in this book.

More experienced musicians, or those who recognize particular needs or gaps in their own experience, may wish to use the book selectively. None the less, it will be advisable to read it through completely first, as many of the concepts and terms introduced in earlier chapters are taken for granted later on.

However the book is used, by large classes led by a tutor, by small groups with or without experienced guidance, or by individuals working privately, it is essential to vary the *pace* and *repetition* of study, particularly in the 'Exercise and discussion' paragraphs and in the 'Do-it-yourself exercises'. Some exercises are described in a sentence or two but may lead to hours of purposeful musical activity. Others are intended to make a point which can be grasped in a flash and, once understood, need never be restated.

Similarly, some exercises need be done only once for a point to be made or a realization to dawn. Others will be useful throughout the active life of any musician, to be repeated and developed every time an instrument is taken from its case or a pencil put to manuscript paper. So every 'exercise' or 'experiment' should be assessed as to how long you should spend on it and how frequently it should be done, to meet your own personal needs. The 'soundscape' experiment in section 2.1 takes only a couple of minutes, and once its point is made it need not be repeated formally, though you should subsequently find yourself more aware of ambient sounds. On the other hand, the exercise in section 2.2 of noticing metrical variation should be a part of your musical awareness for ever, not laboured as when doing the exercise for the first time, but a recurring momentary thought in any musical situation.

Although the 'Exercises and discussions' and 'Do-it-yourself exercises' should serve to exemplify every point and give adequate practice in the skills you are developing, they are intended only as a starting-point. The more you use your imagination to vary and expand them, the better. Some will need changing to suit your own situation. If you are fortunate enough to have access to a great deal of live music, perhaps in a conservatoire or college with an active programme of student concerts, you can use it in preference to frozen performances on record. If much of your spare time is spent in playing in university, college or county orchestras, some of the exercises can be adapted to suit times when you are playing, or sitting through bars' rest, in rehearsals.

However the exercises are done, it is absolutely essential that they are finally returned to a truly musical context. Playing games with timbral perception in a class room or lecture room is no more valuable than writing down anonymous tunes from dictation unless the experience of such games is taken back into your imagination as composer, your interpretation as performer, and your critical appreciation as a listener. Indeed the only justification for a course such as this book outlines is that there simply is not time to deal with its issues fully in rehearsal and practice, in tutorial and lecture, or in a period a week in the school timetable. As a violinist will subject a point of technique to concentrated study with long hours of largely unmusical bowing exercises for example, so a course in aural awareness allows us to pause, to extract an issue from its wider musical context and subject it, for a time, to a higher level of magnification. But such study has no musical value in isolation. It bears fruit, as do the violinist's exercises, only when it is returned to the context of real musical activity.

Where listening to a specific piece would be useful, I have added in square brackets the reference number of a recommended recording. The RED Classical Catalogue, or any co-operative record dealer, will help you to find it, though other recordings will generally serve just as well.

1

Hearing and listening: what is available

1.1 Focusing your ears

To take any active part in music, we have to *perceive* it. This in itself is not as easy as it may appear. For example, as you read this, is any music audible? Perhaps you are in the music department of a university or polytechnic, or in a conservatoire, or in the music block of a school. You may be at home, with background music on as you read—or your next-door-neighbour is practising the sousaphone. . . . But until you are made aware of it, you may well not perceive this music: it is *heard* but not *listened to*.

For another illustration, imagine yourself in a crowded room, perhaps at a party at which people are talking in groups. You are *hearing* all the sounds around you, but *listening* only to the conversation within your own particular group. To use a visual analogy, your own conversation is in focus, the others out-of-focus. If however someone in the neighbouring group mentions your name, your attention will probably be attracted and you will start listening in focus to this second conversation which you had previously heard only out of focus and subconsciously.

Exercise and discussion

Discuss the music you hear, both in and out of focus, during a typical working day. Make a diary of such a day, beginning perhaps with an alarm-clock radio, continuing through the background music from radio or breakfast television, from 'Muzak' in shops and from buskers in streets, from personal stereos secreted within your clothing—and so on throughout the day, until the Open University fanfare signals the close-down of broadcasting on one television channel at least.

There is a tendency among so-called 'serious' musicians to scorn much of this music as mere 'wallpaper'. Yet wallpaper clearly enhances the quality of our environment. It becomes undesirable only if it is the limit of our visual experience, if the wallpaper obscures the Watteau or the patterns conceal the Picasso. Provided that we can focus at will on 'art' we should not deny ourselves unfocused 'decoration'.

So too with music. Provided we do not lose the ability to focus aurally when we identify something which deserves such close attention, we need not fear unfocused musical sounds around us. The threat may seem to be that they might dull our sensitivity. In fact, as we train our ears and minds to focus attentively, the problem is often rather that we begin to focus on the decorative music, the 'Muzak', too. While others chatter merrily on in a restaurant or bar, trained musicians may find it hard to carry on coherent conversation against the distraction of background music.

1.2 Expanding musical awareness

Once music is *perceived*, musicians then need to be able to *analyse* and *identify* the elements within it. Much conventional aural training is concerned with the analyses and identification of pitches and durations—some were listed in the Introduction. One of the aims of this book is to expand the range of musical elements of which we are conscious, to add to such pitch-based skills as recognizing intervals or cadences others like the tone-qualities of instruments, and how a composer's notation and a performer's technique can control them.

For all this perception, both conventional and any which may come to your attention for the first time as you read on, the sheer amount of music around us is of tremendous advantage. 'Aural awareness' can be developed all the time, everywhere. To limit your training to, say, an hour's class once a week when studying music seriously—in sixth form, degree or diploma courses—is hopelessly inadequate. With the amount of music available, such as you will have listed for the exercise in section 1.1, aural opportunity is everywhere around us, for many hours a day. In later chapters you will constantly be urged to apply ideas, first examined in isolation, to every musical situation in which you find yourself: to listen actively rather than simply *practise* on 'autopilot'; to focus intently on the quality of sounds made by those around you in *ensembles* such as orchestras, choirs and bands; to identify particular parts of *concert* programme to listen to at a level of intensity which could probably not be sustained continuously through a whole two-hour performance.

Exercise and discussion

For now, consider the range of listening opportunities which exists even in non-musical everyday life for those inquisitive enough to look for them. Discuss in groups of three, if you are working in a class, aural phenomena which can be relevant to the training of your ears—and brains—for activity in music. Examples might range from very traditional 'interval spotting' occasions to subtle perceptions of timbre; from discovering the intervallic range of an ambulance siren to identifying the specific tone-quality by which your dog recognizes the sound of your family car but ignores others. Collate your ideas in a list, and use it as a stimulus to listen—to anything, at any time during your waking hours.

2

The elements of musical expression

2.1 Analysis and synthesis

The aim in this chapter is to break down the total experience of listening to music into separate elements. You will find the division rather artificial, of course: how can anyone listen to the melodic intervals at the beginning of Beethoven's Fifth Symphony without being conscious of the vigorous rhythmic patterns too? But it is helpful to divide this total experience of listening into its constituent parts, first, to focus attention on them, and second to break down the whole process of analysing music by ear into manageable proportions. Then, as with every thought, every exercise, every experience that we isolate when developing musical awareness, it is essential to put it back immediately into the context of real music. Breaking down the total experience, *analysis*, becomes constructive only when followed by building up again, by *synthesis*. Then, the original listening experience can become greatly heightened. In fact, you will hear things of which you were simply not aware before.

Prove this to yourself now with the simplest of experiments: when you reach the end of this paragraph, put the book down, shut your eyes, and analyse the 'soundscape' around you for a full minute. Then take pencil and paper and jot down a list of what you heard. . . . Now compare notes with others around you, if you are working in a group. . . .

Two interesting things will probably have happened: first, your list will include sounds which were happening all the time but of which you were totally unaware until you did the experiment. You will have noticed the road-drill outside or the trombonist practising next door, but not the breathing of the person sitting next to you, the rumble of distant traffic or the hum of a fluorescent light: sounds which have been audible, but which you did not perceive, a point we examined at the beginning of Chapter 1. Second, there may be differences between your list and that of someone else: even when everyone focuses on one simple sound-scape, we do not necessarily all perceive the same things.

As you end the experiment to *analyse* the surrounding sound-scape, you will then naturally *synthesize* it so that less important sounds recede into the background. You will revert to selective listening. But the experiment has a lasting effect in that you are still aware of the nature of your 'sound environment' even if you are not constantly listening to all the elements which constitute it. Similarly the process of analysing and synthesizing the elements in a piece of music heightens your appreciation of it.

2.2 Metre and rhythm

'Metre' refers to the regular placing of strong and weak beats in a recurring pattern. So '$\frac{4}{4}$ time' is a metre of four beats to a bar, with the first carrying a natural emphasis so that the recurring pattern is discernible.

'Rhythm' refers to the distribution of note values, normally within a metre. Rhythms may be metrical. The hymn by Thomas Tallis, 'Tallis' Canon' (Ex. 2.2a) moves in constant minims throughout.

Ex. 2.2a 'Tallis' Canon', Thomas Tallis (*c.* 1505–85)

13

At the other extreme, rhythms may be virtually unmetrical without bar-lines and with no regularly implied strong beats. C. P. E. Bach wrote Fantasias with no bar-lines, though the note values are grouped in such a way that repeated metrical patterns sometimes appear (Ex. 2.2b).

Ex. 2.2b Fantasia for keyboard, C. P. E. Bach (1714–88)

In between these extremes, the influence of metre on rhythm is infinitely varied, ranging from bar-lines to keep an ensemble of performers together but with instructions such as senza misura ('without measure'), as in the opening 'Procession' of Benjamin Britten's *Ceremony of Carols* (Op. 28) [HYPE CDA66220] and, by contrast, quite clear metrical pulses without any bar-lines in earlier music in particular: Dowland's *Lachrymae or Seaven Teares* [AMON CD-SAR55], complex polyphonic pieces for five viols published in 1604, have no bar-lines in the viol parts yet have a clear ⅔ or ⁴⁄₂ pulse. This then floats free of artificial accents which would be implied by regular bar-lines (Ex. 2.2c).

Ex. 2.2c 'Lachrimae' Pavan, John Dowland (1563–1626)

Rhythms in turn may be uniform, with all the parts moving together in homophonic chords. The voice parts of the 'Hallelujah' chorus from Handel's *Messiah* begin in this way.

Equally, rhythms may be non-uniform, with lines moving independently of each other. This is true of contrapuntal music—every fugue of Bach's '48', *The Well-Tempered Clavier*, has 'voices' which move within a regular metre but with irregular and non-uniform rhythms.

Exercise and discussion

Think of familiar music such as the piece you are currently learning, either alone or in orchestra, band, choir or other group.

15

Consider the most recent recording you have bought or borrowed, be it pop album or classical symphony. Listen to the music of TV adverts. Consider how far any parts of whatever music you choose are

1. metrically regular or irregular
2. rhythmically uniform or non-uniform.

Search, in your own music or in your public or institutional music library, for varieties of rhythmic devices such as composers varying time-signatures to accommodate changing metres (e.g. Stravinsky, Symphony in C, the third movement using, in the first twenty-eight bars, the following succession of time signatures: $\frac{4}{8}, \frac{3}{8}, \frac{4}{8}, \frac{2}{8}, \frac{3}{8}, \frac{2}{8}, \frac{3}{8}, \frac{5}{16}, \frac{3}{8}, \frac{5}{16}, \frac{2}{8}, \frac{5}{16}, \frac{3}{8}, \frac{5}{16}, \frac{7}{16}$); using dotted barlines to guide performers in non-metrical music (much of the notation of Britten's Parable for Church Performance, *Curlew River* (1965) [Schw 313972], is controlled in this way); writing exact note values but requiring rhythmic freedom in performance (e.g. recitative in any Handel opera or oratorio).

If you find your examples in scores, make every effort to hear them, from recordings or by playing them. You need not necessarily achieve a polished performance. Two quite modest keyboard players can play a string quartet as a duet; electronic keyboards and sequencers can allow you to build up a performance line by line.

Equally, if you come across an example from a heard performance, live or on record, try to find a score of it to see how it is notated.

Share and discuss your findings with others studying music with you.

2.3 Pitch

The meaning of 'pitch' is familiar to all. What may be less obvious are the ways in which it is organized. At one extreme music may demand very few different pitches. So children's singing games use as few as three notes—remember the opening of 'Ring-a-ring of Roses'. Much folk music uses a five-note, pentatonic, scale—'Loch Lomond' is an example.

Seven-note scales, organized as major and minor, provide the main body of western tonal music—the first ten bars of the 'Hallelujah' chorus require no more than the seven notes of D major, duplicated at several octaves; a G♯ appears in bar 11. The next chromatic alteration, another G♯, does not appear until bar 26. Our present-day 'major' and 'minor' are just two of the *modes*, ways in which the notes of scales can be ordered. In times past, other orderings of notes were used: the plainchant melody *Dies irae, dies illa* is in the Dorian mode, equivalent to the white notes from D on a keyboard. So too is the sea-shanty 'What shall we do with a drunken sailor', sung as the capstan was turned to raise the anchor.

Vaughan Williams creates a sense of other-worldliness with the same mode in his Symphony No. 5: listen to the violin/flute melody after the opening horn and clarinet calls of the first movement [EMIM CD-EMX9512].

Seven notes suffice for much music in earlier modes, though additional ones arose through the conventions of *musica ficta* whereby performers would for example often raise a flattened leading note at a cadence.

The full western chromatic scale of twelve notes is commonly called on by composers in the seventeenth century—Purcell's *Four-Part Fantasia, No. 5* (1680) [VIRG VC5 45062-2] uses all twelve notes in its first seventeen bars. Just over a century later, Mozart uses eleven out of twelve notes in the first five bars of a staggering unison outburst in his Symphony No. 40 in G minor (K550) after the double bar of the last movement. Look up these examples if you have access to a music library containing some or all of the scores. Listen to them if you can find recordings.

Twentieth-century twelve-note serial music uses all the notes of our chromatic scale, often avoiding giving priority to any one of them, though other music of this century achieves an atonal character without necessarily using all twelve notes.

Intervals of less than a semitone occur in the music of other cultures, notably in South Asia, and from a few western composers, dividing the octave into nineteen, thirty-one or, in the case of Harry Partch, forty-three intervals. Music generated in the electro-acoustic studio can capitalize on the flexibility of

17

electronic instruments and computers to produce variations in pitch as small as the ear can perceive.

More commonly though, variations on the twelve-note scale are by expressive bending of pitch. So, an Indian sitar player uses simple basic scales, or Ragas, of only five, six or seven notes, but stretches the strings to produce nuances of pitch beyond them. Folk singers and pop guitarists and vocalists do the same to some extent—and any performer whose instrument is capable of pitch variation will use that facility, from the controlled vibrato of a classical violinist to the exhilarating glissandi of a jazz clarinettist.

Exercise and discussion

Again referring to music with which you are currently involved, consider how it uses pitch—how many different pitches are present and how they are organized, in major or minor scales or in historical modes for example. If you are playing the second tenor viol part of Purcell's *Fantasia upon One Note* (*c.* 1680) [VIRG VC5 45062-2] you will have no variation of pitch at all unless you introduce an unstylistic vibrato. A Chopin nocturne will involve areas of seven-note scales, changing as the key-centre changes, and with some additional chromatic colouring. So will a song by George Gershwin.

Again, share and discuss your findings with fellow musicians.

2.4 Texture

Texture refers to the way in which lines of music relate to each other both vertically and horizontally. So, the 'voices' of a Bach fugue, melodically independent of each other though making coherent vertical harmony together, create a polyphonic texture or counterpoint. The 'voices' of a hymn, on the other hand, move largely simultaneously to create a homophonic texture of successive chords.

In between these two extremes, there is a great variety of intermediate textures such as a decorated melody flowing above accompanying chords. The chords in turn may be homophonic or broken up in 'Alberti' patterns. Exs. 2.4a, 2.4b, 2.4c and 2.4d

Ex. 2.4a Fugue in A minor, from '48' Book II, J. S. Bach (1685–1750)

Ex. 2.4b *Variations*, Op. 27, Anton Webern (1883–1945)

Ex. 2.4c 'The Chrysanthemum', Scott Joplin (1868–1917)

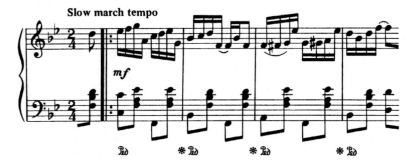

are four varieties of texture ranging from the independence of counterpoint to the simultaneous sounding of notes in homophonic chords. Play them.

Furthermore, we can influence our perception of texture by the way in which we choose to listen to it. For example, we can

Ex. 2.4d 'Ce moys de may', Clément Jannequin (*c.* 1475–*c.* 1560)

Ce moys de may, ce moys de may, ce moys de may, ma ver - te cot-te

hear the alto part of a hymn as a contrapuntal line if we decide to concentrate upon its melodic quality rather than perceive it only as a series of notes contributing to successive vertical chords.

Exercise and discussion

Re-examine some of the music you have looked at for the exercise and discussion at the end of section 2.3, but this time considering its various textures. Compare notes with other students so that your collection of textures is as wide as possible.

2.5 Timbre

Timbre, or tone-colour, is a quality which we can all perceive at its more apparent levels. No musician could confuse the timbre of a string quartet with that of a brass band. To this extent, although few people have 'perfect pitch', that is the ability to recognize pitch without any given reference points, we all have 'perfect timbre'. Nor does the more subtle comparison of, say, flute and oboe normally confuse us unless exceptional players are using the extremes of their 'timbral spectrum' to make one instrument sound like the other.

Timbre also varies across the range of a single instrument. The thick, weighty open G string of a violin has a different *quality* as well as a different *pitch* from the thin metal E string; the clarinet has a quality in its bottom register which is so audibly charac-

20

teristic that it bears the name, 'chalumeau', of the clarinet's ancestor.

A third level of timbral variation is that within a single note. It may be achieved by alternative fingerings—'sul G' on the violin, where the player reaches high positions on the G string rather than using the higher strings, or an alternative fingering on a wind instrument perhaps to facilitate a difficult passage. Bowing techniques, tonguing, vibrato, and the quality of the instrument—and the player—all contribute to a virtually infinite range of timbres, the subject of detailed study in instrumental and singing lessons but seldom touched on in traditional 'aural training'.

Exercise and discussion

Listen to contrasting recordings of the same or similar music—Beethoven played on a fortepiano and a modern instrument, a Bach *Brandenburg Concerto* movement played on modern orchestral instruments and by an early music ensemble using authentic instruments. Concentrating *only* on timbre, write down a few comments and then compare notes with the observations of others in the group.

Listen to a recording of the second movement of the String Quartet No. 4 by Béla Bartók [ASV CDDCS301]. As it flies by at breathtaking speed, you can hear normal 'arco' bowing, pizzicato plucking, harmonics, and 'sul ponticello'—a quiet rasping sound near the bridge. The following movement, no. III, contrasts 'non-vibrato' with 'vibrato'; moves quickly, in an 'Agitato' section, towards and away from the bridge; and ends with all but first violin muted. Key Stage 3 of the National Curriculum refers to timbral qualities of this kind, though Bartók presents them in such a fast-changing kaleidoscope of colours that you will need several listenings, and perhaps the visual cue of a score, to map each one as it appears.

2.6 Compass, range and density

'Compass' refers to the extent and usable limits of a single instrument or voice, from its highest note to its lowest. So the

21

compass of a bassoon is B♭ to b♭', with occasional extension up to f″ by composers making specially taxing demands on virtuoso performers.

Within the concept of 'compass' is 'register'—the part of the overall compass which is actually being used at any one time. For some instruments, registers are quite specific and characteristic. So, for example, the clarinet has a warm 'chalumeau' register at the lower end and a brilliant 'clarino' register at the top.

'Range' refers not to the instrument but to the demands of the music; the range of voices singing plainchant is narrow, while that of one of the solo instruments in a few bars from Bach's Concerto for Two Violins (BWV 1043) is fairly large (Ex. 2.6a).

Within this notation of 'range' is also the spacing of notes. So, for instance, within the seven octaves of a piano keyboard, the three notes C, C♯ and D may be spread over a wide range (Ex. 2.6b) or clustered together over a narrow range (Ex. 2.6c), and at different points over the piano's compass (Exs. 2.6d and 2.6e).

Ex. 2.6a Plainchant melody 'Veni Creator Spiritus'

Ve-ni Cre - a-tor— Spi- ri-tus, Men-tes tu-o-rum— vi-si-ta: Im-ple—

su - per - na— gra-ti-a Quae— tu cre - a-sti —— pec-to-ra.

Concerto for Two Violins (BWV 1043) (first movement), J. S. Bach (1685–1750)

Vivace

22

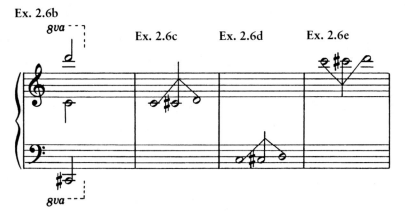

Ex. 2.6b
Ex. 2.6c
Ex. 2.6d
Ex. 2.6e

The clustering or spreading out of notes also creates 'density', though this is influenced particularly by how many notes are sounding. So, a six-note chord is denser than a three-note triad. Density is also affected by compass: play a triad in close position near the bottom of a piano, where it will sound very thick and turgid while the same triad in the treble range sounds quite transparent. Three tubas create a denser sound than three cornets.

'Density' also serves to describe the complexity of a sound: the strings of a full symphony orchestra will play a given chord more densely than will a chamber ensemble; many instruments playing a single note in unison are denser than a single instrument playing that note.

'Tessitura' refers to the part of a range which is used most frequently. Although the ranges of Exs. 2.6f and 2.6g are identical, their tessituras are very different; Ex. 2.6f is much more taxing to sing than Ex. 2.6g.

Ex. 2.6f 'The Ploughboy', William Shield (1748–1829)

When lol-ling in my cha-riot   so   great a man I'll be

'Compass', 'range', density and 'tessitura' are not words universally understood to have distinct and specific meanings when applied to music. We suggest these general definitions simply to

23

The elements of musical expression

Ex. 2.6g *Messiah*, G. F. Handel (1685–1759)

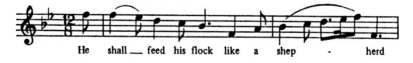

have an agreed vocabulary through which to communicate our sensation as we listen.

Exercise and discussion

Listen three times (together, if you are working in a group) to three contrasting fragments of music. One minute of each may well suffice. Concentrate first on the *range* of a single line—a pop singer's voice, a continuo bass line. At the next hearing, consider *tessitura*—the parts of the range most frequently used. Finally, concentrate on *density*—both how many instruments are playing and over how many different notes they are distributed.

Share your conclusions and discuss any points which were not hit upon by everyone.

2.7 Dynamics

'Dynamics' refers, of course, to loudness and quietness. But these are not absolute levels of volume: a sudden moment of *mf* in a pianissimo passage will appear loud while exactly the same brief *mf* may be almost inaudible if our ears are adjusted to a sustained passage of fortissimo.

Dynamics are also related to timbre—the tone quality of a note played loud is usually quite different from that of the same note played softly.

Another simple experiment will prove this. Play a recording of a passage of loud music with the volume turned down, and a passage of quiet music with the volume turned up. You are very unlikely to have any doubts about which is which. The loud music will sound distant but still have a 'forte' timbre; the quiet music will still sound like quiet music, but close to you, or unnat-

24

urally amplified. With half a dozen examples prepared, one CD-player operator could challenge the rest of the group to specify the composers' dynamic markings of music which is being played too loud, correctly, or too quiet on a sequence of CDs.

Lastly, dynamic variations in music are not only on a wide scale—eight bars of forte and eight of piano, say. Short phrases have natural dynamic subtleties and shadings. Sing the first line of the British National Anthem: almost inevitably the word 'gracious' will be louder than 'save our' and 'Queen'. In fact, 'gra . . .' may be louder than '. . . cious', and the 'g . . .' may have a slight guttural explosion in the throat making it the loudest sound in the word.

So dynamics, on the smallest scale, play a crucial role in articulation.

2.8 Articulation

Play Ex. 2.8a on any suitable instrument. Sing it, too.

Ex. 2.8a *Dido and Aeneas*, Henry Purcell (1659–95)

The first question which arises about the articulation of your performance is very basic indeed: in what metre did you play or sing? In other words, where did you place articulatory *stresses*? Some possibilities include Exs. 2.8b, 2.8c and 2.8d.

Ex. 2.8b

Ex. 2.8c

25

Ex. 2.8d

Hazard a guess as to which Purcell wrote—and do not read on until you have committed yourself . . . !

In fact Belinda, Dido's sister, sings with another woman 'Fear no danger to ensue, The hero loves as well as you'. Fit these words to Ex. 2.8a and, probably unexpectedly, you discover that Purcell wrote in $\frac{3}{4}$ time, as indicated in Ex. 2.8c.

Articulation is, therefore, partly a matter of *stress*, which normally implies a brief increase in dynamic level. But half way through this fragment of music there is a comma in the words— '. . . to ensue, the hero . . .'—so the eight bars are articulated in two equal halves, divided by a momentary silence and, probably, a breath for the singer. So here articulation involves a momentary silence as well as a series of stresses.

'Danger' is set to ♩ ♩♩ (Ex. 2.8e) so the second syllable requires two legato notes: the most markedly contrasting kinds of articulation are staccato and legato, and each of these in turn can be at various degrees from a very detached molto staccato through tenuto to a legato so smooth as to be a continuous strand of uninterrupted sound.

Performers sing this duet with widely varying degrees of articulation, from a bounding separation of each syllable from the next to a lilting legato with a momentary break after four bars. If you played it on an instrument, ignoring the implications of the words, you could range from fiercely tongued/spiccato bowed detachment to a total legato throughout. Try it.

But now you know it is in $\frac{3}{4}$ time, you would find it hard not to hint, at least, at an articulation of its metre by a slight stress after each bar-line of Purcell's original melody, Ex. 2.8f.

Exercise and discussion

Listen to any piece of music focusing your concentration *only* upon the broader sweeps of dynamic variation. Then listen to a

Ex. 2.8f

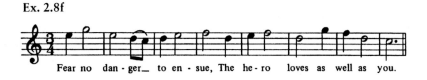

Fear no dan - ger— to en - sue, The he - ro loves as well as you.

few bars of it again, this time to identify the smallest nuances of dynamic, creating rhythmic clarity and phrasing.

Finally, repeat this, several times if you wish, until your ears have assessed every accent, every moment of silence, every bite of a bow or explosion behind a tongue—the techniques which combine to create articulation.

Note down what you hear, and discuss your findings with others, if you are working in a group.

2.9 Placing in space

Where sounds come from can profoundly influence how we hear them. Try two simple experiments.

First, play a stereo recording of a piece of orchestral music, the more spacious the better. The opening of Richard Strauss's *Also sprach Zarathustra* [PHIL 442 281-2] or of Wagner's *Mastersingers* overture [EMI CDC5 55479-2] are good examples. Then switch to 'mono' if your CD equipment has this facility or, alternatively, turn the 'balance' control fully to left or right so that sound is coming from only one speaker. Immediately you will notice that, as the breadth from which the sound comes narrows to a single point, it loses clarity of detail. The texture and individual tone qualities of, say, violins and 'cellos are much more easily heard if they are separated, violins on the left, 'cellos on the right. The contrasting timbres of flute and bassoon heard across the breadth of an orchestra are much more clearly discernible than if they fuse together in a single point in space— as a 'boot' or a 'flassoon', perhaps!

Second, have two people standing one immediately behind the other and saying something simultaneously, such as 'This is an experiment in placing sound in space'. The two voices will be far

27

less individually distinguishable than the same two speaking in unison from opposite sides of the room. Try it out.

Exercises

First, have two or three players of the same instrument (recorder, flute, violin . . .) each play a different sustained note, repeatedly. The remainder of the group should each select one of the performers to concentrate upon. Listeners then close their eyes, while the players walk about, playing their respective notes. Listeners concentrate on where their chosen players are in the room. If the players play the *same* note, this can become a very sophisticated exercise in recognizing different timbres. When you have followed a note around the room, by ear and with eyes closed, it is amusing as well as instructive to find, as you open your eyes, whether you have kept in aural touch with the right person.

Second, another way of making yourself aware of space is to move around in it yourself. If you are working as a group and the room is large enough for a space to be cleared of furniture, shuffle around it, humming and with your eyes closed. Pick a specific pitch and tone-quality in which to hum, and avoid bumping into others by hearing their characteristic 'hums' and identifying their positions in the space around you. Experience suggests that it is advisable to have someone, tutor or student volunteer, to supervise with eyes open and warn of such impending accidents as someone blundering out through the door and falling headlong down stairs.

Although these spatial dimensions enhance our listening at live concerts and recitals and, to a lesser extent, when we hear recordings in well-balanced stereo, we frequently ignore the placing of music in space as we use our 'inner hearing', as we *imagine* sound. Think to yourself the opening two bars of Beethoven's Fifth Symphony. . . . Did you hear the *breadth* of the sound as well as the familiar rhythm and the falling third?

Similarly when reading music silently, we tend to miss its expansiveness. Do you read a full orchestral chord simply as a pillar of vertical sound, or does your imagination have horns on

28

the left and trombones on the right? Or perhaps you are sitting in the cheapest seats, on the platform behind the orchestra—in which case the placing of horns and trombones will be reversed.

2.10 Pace

The pace at which musical events occur is a crucial element in the character of that music. A constant rhythm for a long period of time creates a quite different musical effect from that of frequent changes of rhythm. Fast changes of harmony contrast with slow. A composer may retain one timbre over a long period—a whole movement or more of a Bach harpsichord suite—or change tone colour constantly in a complex web of orchestration such as a movement of a Mahler symphony. (Listen to one of each if you have recordings available.) What is more, the *pace* at which these changes occur may have no relation whatsoever to the tempo ('allegro', 'andante', 'largo') of the music.

So it is important to be aware not only of variations in rhythm, pitch, timbre, compass, range and so on, but also of the pace at which these variations are happening.

2.11 Structure

Structure refers to the ways in which music is organized within formal moulds, from the smallest scale to the largest. We shall examine this in some detail later, in Chapter 8. For now, we use the term to describe such small-scale organization as repetitions of a motive, a bar, a phrase, or near repetitions such as sequences. The balancing of two bars with another two, or four with four, is structural as is the musical architecture of large-scale forms such as binary or ternary, sonata form, or the familiar classical pattern of a minuet surrounding a trio, with all their customary repeats.

Exercise and discussion

Listen to two short and contrasted pieces of music. A classical minuet and trio and a current piece of pop music would be

29

suitable. Hear each several times and jot down any observations you may have to make about the *pace* at which events occur: how frequently does the dynamic level change, for example, and how fast are the changes of harmony? Then, giving yourself further hearings, note any *structural* features: is every moment of the music new, for example, or does it repeat, either exactly or with some variation? Can you predict when it is going to end? If so, why?

All these exercises are best done in groups, so that you can test ideas and share them immediately. However, do not on any account limit your thinking about all these musical elements solely to timetabled hours in a music course. What begin as 'exercises' should quickly become instinctive ways of responding to any music you hear which, in society today, can be with you almost constantly through radio, personal stereo and background 'Muzak'—great blessings when used creatively.

3

Aural synthesis

3.1 Musical effects

So far, we have identified a selection of elements of musical expression. By concentrating on them one at a time we may begin to see the influences at work to give a piece of music its unique character. But it is not enough merely to observe that a selection of elements is occurring: we need in addition to become aware of the *effect* of that occurrence. Furthermore, musical character depends not on individual elements alone but on the ways in which they interact. The aesthetic experience of music requires more than simply an objective recognition of its constituent parts.

So in this chapter we shall begin to investigate the EFFECTS created by the elements, the EFFECTORS, and the ways in which they interact upon each other.

3.2 The raw materials

To begin with, a check-list of elements will be useful:

1. Metre—underlying pulse; regular or varying.
2. Rhythms—uniform or non-uniform.
3. Pitch—pentatonic (or fewer notes); seven notes, major, minor or modal; polytonal; twelve notes, tonal or atonal; micro-tonal.

31

4. Texture—independent lines of counterpoint or homophonic block chords, with every stage between.
5. Timbre—varying between instruments; within an instrument; within a single note.
6. Compass—the possible notes of an instrument or voice.
7. Range—the actual notes of a piece of music, within which is Tessitura—the most frequently used part of the range.
8. Density—the number, distribution and doubling of notes.
9. Dynamics—both broad and detailed.
10. Articulation—the degree of accent and separation of notes, motives and phrases.
11. Placing in space—where one or many sounds come from.
12. Pace—how frequently any or all of the elements above occur and change.
13. Structure—within what small- and large-scale moulds musical events are organized.

If you can memorize these thirteen 'elements' they will serve as a list to flip through in your mind, at least until your musical awareness is developed enough for you to be certain that all would occur to you as a matter of course. You may also identify other kinds of musical events which you would want to add to the list. It is not intended to be wholly inclusive.

3.3 Effectors and effects

Having extracted each element from its musical context and examined it by analysis, it must be put back into context again, or synthesized, to discover its effect.

Such 'synthesis' could be of extreme complexity. At the risk of grossly over-simplifying it, consider two concepts, each summarized by two words:

Expansion and *contraction* are EFFECTORS—they make effects happen.
Tension and *release* are EFFECTS—stimulating human responses to what is happening.

So, an *expansion* of dynamic level from a long period of mezzo-piano to a climactic forte is an objective EFFECTOR. Its subjective EFFECT would be to create increased *tension*. But after a lengthy fortissimo or even an exceptionally soft and poignant pianissimo, that same forte might create the EFFECT of *release*.

An EFFECTOR, like the *contraction* of note values from minims through crotchets to quavers or beyond, might have the EFFECT of increasing *tension*. Yet a long note with a pause, an *expanding* note value, can equally create *tension*.

So these concepts and this vocabulary—the effectors, 'contraction' and 'expansion', and their resulting effects, 'tension' and 'release'—are never absolute. They depend on context, on expectations, on the style of particular historical periods. The interval of a seventh is unthinkable within a line of melody by Palestrina; the same interval is part of the characteristic melodic language of Elgar.

The concepts and vocabulary depend too on your personal reaction to musical stimulus. No two aural analyses and synthe-ses of an extended piece of music will be identical, as we shall now see.

Exercise and discussion

Draw eight generously spaced bar-lines on a piece of blank paper. Then listen, half a dozen times or more, to the first eight bars of, say, Mozart's Symphony No. 39 in E♭ (K543). (As the following discussion and examples are based on this music, you should try to obtain a suitable recording, or two if possible [EMI CMS7 63856-2; ARCH 447 043-2].)

As you listen, use graphic notations to analyse what is hap-pening. Some notation will be conventional—'*f*' is the most con-venient way of notating the fact that a passage of music is loud. A very few people have 'perfect pitch' and can write musical notation easily. For most, simply a graphic sign showing how relatively high or low is pitch, and in what direction it is moving, is sufficient. Make a note, too, of the combinations of pitch cre-ating harmony; all that is needed is to be aware of the pace of harmonic change and the tension which harmonies create. So the first harmony (actually the tonic chord) contrasts with the second which has moved away from tonic repose to dominant

33

tension. Rhythms may best be sketched in conventional notation. The available 'timbral spectrum' is probably best noted by
listing the instruments you hear at the beginning of your 'score';
you may need to invent symbols for the most subtle variations in
timbre not specified by Mozart but arising from the artistry of
the players.

Constantly glance through the check-list on pp. 31–32, deciding which of the first eleven *elements* are operating at any one
time, and at what *pace* they are being manipulated. Finally, consider how the *expansion* and *contraction* of EFFECTORS creates EFFECTS of increased *tension* and the opposite, its *release*.

There are no right or wrong 'answers' to this exercise. Even an
exact reproduction of the printed score omits the minute variations of metre, timbre, dynamics and articulation which define
a phrase. Mozart uses only two dynamic markings, *f* and *p*, but
you will probably hear many variations within each of these.

Everyone's score will differ, so discuss yours with others, in
groups of two or three. Add to your score anything suggested by
others, once you have agreed that an element was present and
how it was used to create an effect. You may well disagree. All
the better: we all respond differently to stimuli of all kinds, not
only musical ones.

After ten minutes of discussion and modification of your
graphic scores, hear the eight bars again once or twice, to give
you a final opportunity to change your mind—or confirm a dog-
matically held opinion.

Ex. 3.3a suggests a very few of the elements you may have
observed, and how they are used as effectors to create effects.
The exact notation is printed here only for convenience—*your
score will almost certainly not contain most of the pitched notes*,
though you might have noted the tempo, 'adagio', the clefs
appropriate to the instruments, the time signature and some
phrasing slurs.

One conclusion which you might have come to is that the first
and third pairs of bars, 1–2 and 5–6, are exactly the *same* as each
other in terms of *every single one of the first 11 elements except
pitch*. (Bars 3–4 are also the same except for the missing *piano*
horns.) Then bars 7–8 are totally *different* from the earlier bars

in terms of *all 11 elements except metre.* This astonishing level of contrast only becomes apparent when you consider each element in turn; no wonder the opening of this symphony is such a striking musical gesture.

3.4 Do-it-yourself exercises

The following suggestions are for exercises to do in your own time, as often, as long, and as intensively as you wish.

First, while listening to any music at all on radio or from a recording, concentrate for a few moments on each of the 'elements' listed in section 3.2 in turn. Have available pencil and paper, to jot down any observations that occur to you. This exercise can also be done quite spontaneously. The background 'Muzak' in a shop or restaurant is as useful a source of sound as a carefully selected cassette tape or CD. So too is the music of television jingles or the incidental music to a film.

Second, do a similar exercise in focusing on elements, one by one, in part of your instrumental or vocal practice. As you sing or play a phrase, how flexible is the metre, the rhythm, the dynamics, the articulation . . . ? At what pace do harmonies or note values change at a given point . . . ?

Third, again focus on musical 'elements' but in a live concert or recital. It need not be a formal occasion; if you have a friend with whom to work, you can play a brief recital to each other.

In all these exercises, it is important to write down your observations. Nothing clarifies a vague thought like the discipline of putting it into words.

Finally, share as many of these experiences with others as you can. Two or three students working together will not only make more observations than one working alone, but will also stimulate each other to deeper levels of awareness.

3.5 Group discussions

Certainly, at the next meeting of a group of students studying together, there should be extensive discussion. Talk in groups of

Ex. 3.3a Symphony No. 39 in E♭ (K543), W. A. Mozart (1756–91)

three, rather than larger groups in which some will dominate while others are afraid to speak. Have two people asking challenging and penetrating questions about the observations being described by the third. If one describes hearing the timbral quality of an oboe, the others might press for details—was it a baroque oboe or a modern one? Was it a thin or reedy sound? Did the player have a strongly characteristic sound such as a French vibrato?

After a few minutes, reverse the roles so that one of the questioners becomes the questioned.

3.6 Varied interpretations

If recordings are available, there is more to be done with the opening of the Mozart symphony too. With your own 'graphic' score in front of you, and the printed score (Ex. 3.3a) listen to two contrasting recordings of the first eight bars. The greater the contrast the better; the developing taste for performances on period instruments has produced sounds which differ very markedly from those of large symphony orchestras. (The recordings suggested in 3.3 are very different from each other.)

Here there will be no differences in relative pitches (though an 'authentic' performance may be at a different overall pitch). Nor will there be metrical differences. So these issues, pitch and metre, which tend to dominate conventional 'aural training', will not arise at all. There will, however, be differences in every one of the remaining elements listed in section 3.2, and in the way they are manipulated, by expansion and contraction, as effectors creating effects—tension and release. Note them, on paper, on your graphic score or on Ex. 3.3a, using different coloured pens for each interpretation.

Finally, after as many hearings as you need to observe the differences without simply becoming bored with the repetition, compare notes, in groups of three of course.

3.7 Expanding the repertoire

These exercises can now be done with any music you please, analysing and synthesizing both single performances and pairs of contrasting interpretations on record. Some will yield a complex range of sounds, varying at a bewildering pace. Others—a minuet for keyboard or a part of a repetitive 'minimalist' piece—will involve more subtle musical effects, made all the more striking by their restraint.

Always limit the amount you hear to manageable proportions. Four bars absorbed, analysed and synthesized thoroughly are worth far more, for the purposes of training yourself in aural perception, than forty bars which drift past you simply as an agreeable sensation. Indeed, all the exercises above should be made short enough to be done successfully. Only extend them as your awareness deepens, as your musical memory improves, and as your confidence in your powers of aural perception increases.

There is no limit to the music available for you to work with as the skills in analysis can be applied to any music, from any period, for any medium. However, when applying these skills to less familiar music than that of the mainstream western tonal tradition, emphases will be different. Take as an example *Threnody for the Victims of Hiroshima* (1960) by the Polish composer Krzysztof Penderecki [CONI CDCF 168]. The opening of this is reproduced as Ex. 3.7a (pp. 43–45), *but do not turn to it yet* as it provides answers to many of the aural questions you should be asking yourself as you listen to it. (It is available in several recordings.)

Play 1 minute and 49 seconds of the opening of *Threnody . . .* , several times.

Check through the list of 'elements' in your mind and jot down an assessment of their roles in the piece. For example, it is clearly not *metrical* in the conventional sense of there being an audible pulse, so many beats to a bar. Nor is it *rhythmical* in the conventional sense that note values are combined to fill out the first bar of the Mozart Symphony No. 39 (K543). Yet there are rhythms on a much broader scale, created by broad changes in timbres and textures. You might ask yourself how performers keep together in an ensemble like this. Does a conductor beat a metre, or simply signify the passing of time? There is much variety of *pitch*, yet it does not create single lines of melody combining either homophonically or in counterpoint. What instruments are used to create these *textures* and *timbres*? How many are there? How much of their *compass* is used by the *range* of the music? What *articulations* and playing techniques are they using to create the sound—accents, vibratos, *dynamic* variations? Map out the variations of *density* during the extract. How, from where you are sitting in relation to stereo loudspeakers, are the instruments placed in *space*? At what *pace* do any of these expressive elements change?

Do not look at Ex. 3.7a until you have spent some time in devising your own graphic score of what you hear, discussing it with others if you are working in a group.

You will probably have come to the conclusion that a piece like *Threnody* . . . does indeed use musical elements common to a Mozart symphony and to anything else you may have listened to, for that matter, but with markedly different emphases. By doing so, Penderecki directs our attention to particular elements which, in other music, are less significant. So, you would recognize the Mozart symphony played on the piano—its pitches (melody and harmony) and its metre and rhythms would be reproduced faithfully enough for it to make musical sense despite a totally different timbre—piano instead of orchestra. The Penderecki piece, on the other hand, depends so much upon timbre and texture, and so little upon exact pitches and an audibly metrical rhythm, that its very essence lies in its orchestration: it is quite untranscribable.

Before leaving *Threnody*, ensure that you hear it all the way through, even if you choose not to continue the exercise of analysing and synthesizing what you hear.

3.8 Do-it-yourself exercises

First, using short, manageable sections from recordings of anything you wish, preferably choosing music for which you have access to a score, make your own analyses and interpretative syntheses. Avoid looking at the score until you have committed yourself to decisions of facts (Are there two flutes? Is it in $\frac{3}{4}$ time? Are the opening notes quavers?) but do not hesitate to use it as the authoritative source of 'right answers' in such matters. However, the score will not help with most of the interpretative matters—does a given rising scale create tension? How much does a conductor vary the metrical pace through a certain phrase?

Second, if you can find two different recordings, make an interpretative analysis of the first, listing each point which occurs to you. Then hear the second recording and consider how it differs or is identical on each of the points you have raised.

Third, listen once to a very brief fragment of music—say, two bars of a $\frac{4}{4}$ Andante. Write down absolutely everything which occurs to you about what you have heard. Listen again three or four times. Reconsider your first conclusions. Do you agree with yourself? If not, how have your opinions changed? Can you explain the changes?

Finally, listen to one of the radio programmes which are concerned with comparisons of recordings. They have titles such as *Building a Library* or *Interpretations on Record* (BBC Radio 3). They often consist of very intense analyses of minute variations in performance—and, incidentally, focus on just those issues which conventional 'aural training' largely omits. Such programmes seldom refer to the pitch of notes or to the metres and rhythms in which they are notated. Rather, they are concerned with interpretational nuances, those manipulations of musical elements which lift a performance of a piece from the prosaic to the sublime.

Ex. 3.7a Abbreviations and symbols

⌐	sharpen a quarter-tone
⌐⌐	sharpen three quarter-tones
♭	flatten a quarter-tone
⌐	flatten three quarter-tones
↑	highest note of the instrument (no definite pitch)
↑	play between bridge and tailpiece
⦀	arpeggio on 4 strings behind the bridge

41

Aural synthesis

T̄	play on the tailpiece (arco) by bowing the tailpiece at an angle of 90° to its longer axis
↑	play on the bridge by bowing the wood of the bridge at a right angle at its right side
⨍	Percussion effect: strike the upper sounding board of the violin with the nut or the finger-tips
⊓ ∨	several irregular changes of bow
⌇⌇⌇	molto vibrato
∿	very slow vibrato with a quarter-tone frequency difference produced by sliding the finger
⤬	very rapid non rhythmicized tremolo
ord.	ordinario
s.p.	sul ponticello
s.t.	sul tasto
c.l.	col legno
l. batt	legno battuto

Ex. 3.7a *Threnody for the Victims of Hiroshima* (1960), Penderecki (1933–)

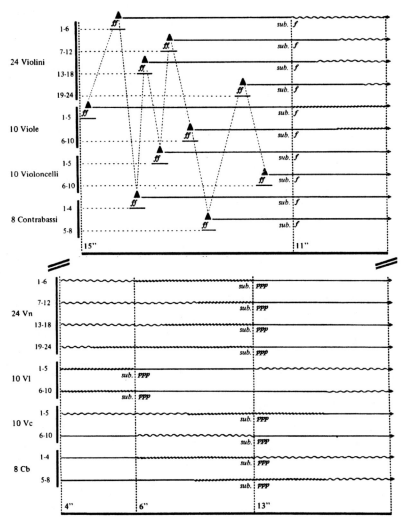

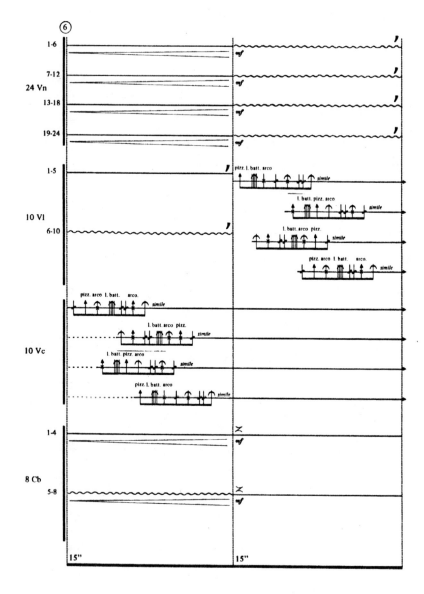

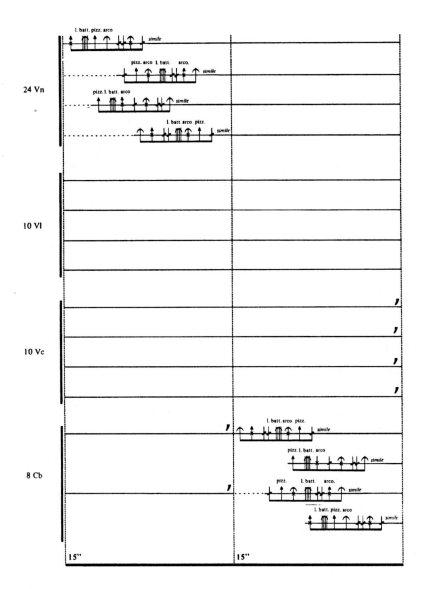

4

Metre and rhythm

4.1 Rhythmic dictation—if you need it

The aim of this chapter is to focus attention on metre and rhythm in the context of real musical activity, be it composing, performing or listening. Before reading further, look again at the definitions of 'metre' and 'rhythm' in section 2.2.

The aim is *not* primarily to develop skill in conventional rhythm dictation which, useful as it may be to specialist transcribers or indeed to composers needing to write down accurately what their imagination 'dictates' to them, can be improved only by repetitive practice. If you need to sharpen up this skill, the most cost-effective way of doing so is outlined in the Introduction: feed yourself two bars—or four, eight or sixteen bars—of a recording, say a minuet from a Haydn string quartet or a nocturne by Chopin. Play as little as you can successfully memorize, as many times as you need, to fix it in your memory. Write it down and compare your manuscript with the authoritatively correct 'answer', the printed score. Every institutional or public library has these resources which can be borrowed for personal use at any time and in any place—in the library itself or on your own hi-fi equipment.

Nevertheless, the exercises in this chapter will help to develop your ability to notate what you hear, and this will be suggested from time to time. Most of the active exercises suggested will require you to think and/or perform up to speed: metre and rhythm cease to evoke their intended musical response from us if they are slowed down or frozen in time. So anything which is finally to be written down *must* first of all be experienced.

4.2 Sharing rhythmic experience

One experience which all performers share is the need to imitate and control metre and rhythms accurately. At its simplest, this may require no more than playing a series of crotchets at a constant pace. Yet, because performance is a human activity, pace is unlikely to be exactly constant. Soloists and chamber musicians, orchestral and choral conductors, rock groups and folk singers all animate their performance with minute degrees of flexibility, with rhythmic nuances.

In ensemble performance it is crucial to respond to such nuances. Individual instrumentalists must, for example, respond to each other's rhythmic initiatives—an oboist may imitate not only the crude notes but also the spontaneous interpretation of the flautist as they share an orchestral motif; the partners of a duo are constantly interacting in metre and rhythm; accurate 'ensemble' of any kind requires exact imitation; even soloists have to 'imitate' physically the creative ideas generated in their own minds.

4.3 Exercises and discussion

First, play a game or two of 'Musical Tennis'. The objectives are to develop your concentration on a steady beat and to listen to others doing the same around you—a skill every musician needs when playing or singing in an ensemble. The rules are simple:

A. Ensemble version.
1. The 'game' is in $\frac{4}{4}$ time.
2. A leader claps for any number of beats, finishing by a click-with-fingers.
3. After the click, the rest of the ensemble claps to complete the bar. The leader takes over again at the start of the next bar.

4. If the leader clicks on the last beat, the ensemble claps a whole bar before the leader takes over again.

So, for example:
(Leader) click, (ensemble) clap, clap, clap
(Leader) clap, click, (ensemble) clap, clap
(Leader) clap, clap, click, (ensemble) clap
(Leader) clap, clap, clap, click, (ensemble) clap, clap, clap, clap
(Leader) clap, . . . etc.

B. The 'tennis' version is a 'singles match' between player 1 and player 2. It is played as above *except* that whenever a click comes *on the fourth (last) beat of a bar*, the 'service' changes, and the other player leads.

So, for example:
(1) clap, clap, click, (2) clap,
(1) clap, clap, clap, *click*,
(2) clap, clap, clap, clap
(still 2) clap, clap, click, (1) clap,
(2) clap, clap, clap, *click*,
(1) clap, etc.

A further development of this game is to play it on instruments, replacing the 'clap' with, say, a bowed note or a specific pitch, and replacing the 'click' with a pizzicato note or one of lower pitch. There will be many 'mishits' (into the net, out-of-court!), to begin with, but as the players become familiar with the rhythm and pulse of the process, and as concentration develops, so too can the pace of the game. Start at crotchet = 60; work up to twice that tempo or more.

Next, within a constant metrical pulse, one person claps or taps to another, or to a whole group, a rhythm—say, four crotchets to begin with—which is then played back in exact imitation. This requires not simply four crotchets but also any minute variation of pace, or of accent, dynamic level, tone quality. These 'effectors', the elements of music, constantly interact to produce musical 'effects' (read again section 3.2). The complexity and the length of the material presented and imitated should gradually

48

be increased. Develop slowly, though; the aim is constant success, not a gradual regression into chaos and demoralization.

Third, extend the challenge by performing/imitating *two* musical units and then repeating them in unison, as in Ex. 4.3a.

Ex. 4.3a

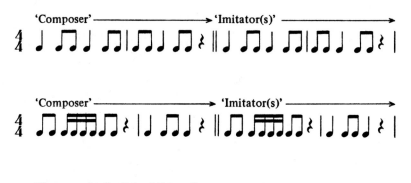

Fourth, write down what you have just 'played'. Compare your score with your neighbour's, using discussion to resolve differences and to diagnose how any mistakes arose.

Finally, agree a pulse of about crotchet = 90. Then have one person clap two or four bars of reasonably simple rhythms such as Ex. 4.3b. Hear the rhythms while *thinking* the metrical pulse.

Ex. 4.3b

Keeping the same pulse going, immediately *imitate* the rhythms, but continue to concentrate your thoughts on the pulse. Still in the context of a continuing pulse, clap crotchets while *thinking* of the rhythms. Then clap the crotchets while verbalizing the

rhythms (i.e. speak them to a syllable such as 'pom'). Finally *verbalize crotchets while clapping the rhythms.*
To summarize:

1. Think crotchets while hearing a rhythmic piece above them.
2. Think crotchets while clapping this rhythmic piece.
3. Think the rhythmic piece while clapping crotchets.
4. Clap crotchets while verbalizing the rhythmic piece.
5. Verbalize crotchets while clapping the rhythmic piece. (You may find this final stage quite exasperatingly difficult!)

Of course, if this proves too complicated, reduce the task—to two bars at a time, to simpler rhythms. Avoid failure: it achieves nothing. Rather, return constantly to this exercise, developing skills slowly, over weeks, months or years.

Two books of games which are invaluable for focusing concentration and developing aural and motor skills are by Trevor Wishart: *Sounds Fun: A Book of Musical Games, No. 1*, Universal Edition, 1990 (ISBN 0900 938 633), and *Sounds Fun 2: A Second Book of Musical Games*, Universal Edition, 1977 (ISBN 0900 938 471). At their simplest, many of these games are playable by pupils of primary school age—they are excellent material for developing the knowledge, skills and understanding required by the National Curriculum. Yet, pushed towards their limits—of tempo, timbral nuance, dynamic variation and the like—they will tax the most sophisticated musicians and generate very concentrated listening as well as great hilarity.

4.4 Rhythm ensembles

The final exercise in section 4.3 can be expanded indefinitely: in length, to six-bar or eight-bar sections or more; in complexity of the rhythms you compose to the metrical pulse; in density, by building up to two or more rhythmic lines against the metre.

The ability to focus on one of several rhythmic lines, or on several at once, is an essential skill for a performer. We do it constantly when playing in ensembles—or, if we do not, the ensemble falls apart. We do it, too, in solo performance. Keyboard players, classical guitarists, harpists actually play interacting lines, but even a solo single-line instrumentalist relates background metre to foreground rhythms. Indeed, the familiar phenomenon of speeding up as rhythms increase in complexity is due to losing contact with the restraining force of an underlying metre.

Composers similarly need to be able to form and retain rhythmic interrelationships in their minds, while the listener who is unaware of such interactions may be receiving only a pale imitation of the riches a composer has to offer.

4.5 The tyranny of the bar-line

So far, the exercises have related rhythms to a regular metrical pulse. This is common to most music, particularly in dance music, where there is normally a regular emphasis on a strong beat or step followed by one, two or three lighter pulses. But that same regular emphasis which may shape the steps of a dance can also inhibit the freedom of music. Ex. 2.2c showed a renaissance Pavan which, while it clearly falls into $\frac{2}{2}$ or $\frac{4}{2}$ time is free from the heavy constraints implied by regular bar-lines. Stravinsky complained of the 'tyranny of the bar-line', which captures and pins down music which could otherwise float free of the implied strong beat which follows it.

All our performance is at times weighed down unnecessarily and detrimentally by the heaviness of the strong beat which starts each bar. It is an illuminating experience to break free of it.

Exercise and discussion

Compose four rhythmic four-bar phrases in $\frac{4}{4}$ time at about crotchet = 120. Avoid, as every good composition should, too many rhythmic motifs. Use repetition, expansion and contraction rather than a new idea at every beat or every bar.

Perform these phrases together as an ensemble, either one-to-a-part or sharing them out around a larger group. Lay a light stress on each first beat as you perform, and extend the piece indefinitely by repeating it.

Once each part is securely learnt, start again. But this time, begin

51

each part one beat later than the previous one. The 'strong' beats
will then no longer coincide, but be distributed equally throughout
the $\frac{4}{4}$ bars. All beats will be 'strong' to one performer or another—
so, paradoxically, no one beat will be stronger than the rest.

Focus your attention, as soon as you feel technically secure in
your performance, not on your own line with every first beat
strong, but on the whole ensemble with no beat stronger than
any other. The resulting freedom from the 'tyranny of the bar-
line' may prove an experience to apply to your performing of
more conventional music.

Ex. 4.5a Huddersfield University Music Students, 1988

Ex. 4.5a shows a composition by first-year degree students
based on rhythm patterns derived from their names. Perform it.
The avoidance of a unanimous strong beat characterizes some of
the more sophisticated kinds of music based primarily on
rhythm. Examples can be found in A. M. Jones, *Studies in
African Music* (Oxford, 1959), and the contemporary minimalist composer, Steve Reich, has transcribed a couple more, from
Ghana, in *Writings on Music* (Halifax, Nova Scotia, 1974).

Exs. 4.5b and 4.5c show two African rhythm-complexes. Play
them, using any instruments which will give you suitably differ-
entiated tone qualities. Clapping, and tapping different materials, will suffice.

Ex. 4.5b Instrumental lines of Sogo Dance from the Ewe tribe, Ghana (after A. M. Jones, *Studies in African Music*)

1 = Gankogui—a two-note bell
2 = Axatse—a two-pitch rattle
3 = Clapping
4 = Clapping
5 = Atsimevu, Master drum, with three distinct tone qualities
6 = Kidi—a two-pitch drum

Ex. 4.5c Four simple drum rhythms with their strong beats out of phase (after A. M. Jones, *Studies in African Music*)

Compose some similar rhythmic counterpoints of your own, consisting of short repeated patterns, each with its own 'downbeat' out of synchronization with the others. Interesting rhythmic counterpoints can be created from the simplest of materials.

Ex. 4.5d

Take a single rhythmic line such as Ex. 4.5d and begin by playing it in unison.

Then divide into two groups. One group continues to play the rhythmic line, while the other plays first in unison a couple of times, then beginning a crotchet late. Continue to gain a final crotchet rest every second playing until, after eight such changes, you are back in unison again. This can also be performed as a do-it-yourself exercise if you first record the unchanging rhythmic line on to tape.

Steve Reich has devised such a rhythmic 'de-synchronization' called simply 'Clapping Music' [COLL 1287-2].

4.6 Do-it-yourself exercises

First, in ensemble rehearsals of choir, orchestra, rock group, recorder consort—or anything else—focus your attention on metre and assess how rigidly or flexibly it is being adhered to. Write your observations down: do not be satisfied with vague generalized conclusions.

Second, spend some time in your private practice *stressing* strong first beats, and then *avoiding* stress on these beats. After exaggerating, decide where, in the piece you are currently learning, such accents and such avoidance of accents might enhance your interpretation.

4.7 Judging speed

Every musician needs to be able to judge speed. Composers indicate their tempo intentions, performers respond to them, and critical listeners judge and appreciate the result.

Within the broad bands of such tempo indications as 'allegro' or 'grave', many performers react intuitively. Yet intuition is clearly unreliable—otherwise why can such a wide range of tempi be chosen by different performers attempting to present the composer's intention for a given piece. Of two recorded performances, particularly of earlier music, one may be more than twice as fast as the other.

J. N. Maelzel patented the metronome in 1814, since when composers have had a means of communicating their intentions absolutely precisely, though even they often change their minds about tempi when they hear aloud and in the concert hall what was previously locked away in their imagination.

Granted that the choice of speed may vary, it is none the less immensely valuable to be able to judge it and relate it accurately to a standard way of notating it in MM (Maelzel's Metronome) numbers. There are several tricks which will guide you to a reasonable approximation of MM speeds. One is borrowed from photographers, measuring seconds of exposure in a darkroom by saying briskly but without gabbling: 'Kodak-1, Kodak-2, Kodak-3' etc.

This gives a pretty good approximation to minim = 60, crotchet = 120 and quaver = 240, thus

Ex. 4.7a

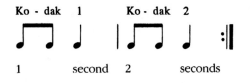

Another verbalization divides a second into three, namely

Ex. 4.7b

One thou - sand   two thou - sand

so crotchet = 180 and, with different barring,

55

'one thou/-sand two/ thou-sand'
minim = 90.

Between them, these two devices should serve to create a reference point when, for example, nervousness makes your mind go blank just before you begin to play or conduct in a public concert.

4.8 Exercises and discussion

First, pick a MM number, tap it out, and measure your accuracy against a metronome.

Second, have someone set a metronome in motion. Judge the MM number at which it is set. This can be developed into a light-hearted competition. Award one mark for an answer within five of the exact number set, two marks for a precisely correct answer assuming, of course, that the challenger selects conventional numbers, crotchet = 90 for example. Crotchet = 89 or 91 would be patently unfair!

Third, invite one instrumentalist to play a passage, lasting about thirty seconds, from a piece in their repertoire. Discuss a suitable MM number for it, experimenting with a metronome. The performer should then play it again, with the metronome set too fast by ten, and again with it set too slow by ten. Discuss the ways in which this affects the performance. It may create technical problems, change the character of articulations, affect convenient breathing or bowing, influence the flexibility of metre—indeed change the musical effect entirely.

Finally, invite an instrumentalist to experiment in front of the rest of the group by playing, accompanied by an audible metronome, first, very strictly metronomically, and second, with exaggerated rubato, but still arriving at new phrases at the moment indicated by the metronome's tick. Again, discuss the musical effects of these two extremes.

4.9 Do-it-yourself exercises

All the exercises in section 4.8 can be done with only a metronome for company; the final one is particularly important.

You should constantly consider the flexibility of your playing within a secure metrical pulse (a development of the skill of attending to two different rhythmic events at once, as in section 4.4). Exaggeration beyond desirable flexibility or rigidity will drive home to you how powerfully manipulation of the *effectors* of metre and rhythm can create *effects* in performance.

4.10 Rhythmic 'imaging'

So far, most of the experiments and exercises in this chapter have begun with the aural experience itself and have then continued with thoughts and discussion about it. An alternative and equally valuable approach is to imagine, or 'image', first and experience after.

Exercise and discussion

Read silently a score of music which is also available on record. Take a simple extract—a two-part keyboard dance or a single-line piece such as one of Britten's *Six Metamorphoses after Ovid* for solo oboe. No. 3, 'Niobe' [HYPE CDA 66776] (Ex. 4.10a), is probably manageable for university/conservatoire students. Less experienced musicians could take, say, a hymn tune, a folk melody, or the first-violin part of a minuet from a string quartet by Haydn. Almost anything will serve, so long as you have both score and recording.

Read the rhythms of the notes within the metre of the time-signature and any tempo indication which may be given. Think particularly about the subtleties of rhythmic flexibility you may expect a performer to add to the relatively inflexible notation. Note that you can ignore all the other musical 'elements' except in so far as they will influence the performance of rhythm and metre. A climax in pitch may imply a delay; a downward scale might accelerate.

Discuss—argue—about your expectations. Note them with suitable graphic symbols on the score: ← can imply holding back, → a slight forward impulse.

Finally, hear a recording of the chosen piece two or three times

Ex. **4.10a** 'Niobe', No. 3 from *Six Metamorphoses after Ovid*, Benjamin Britten (1913–76)

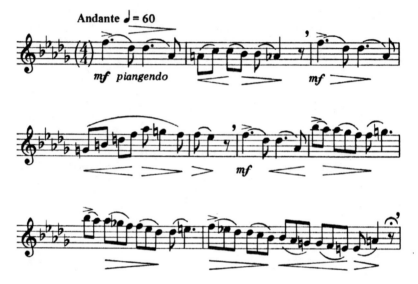

and discuss how far your anticipations were realized. If they were not, you may wish to comment, both favourably and otherwise, on the performance. Judgements like these are not the prerogative only of professional music critics.

4.11 Wider applications

Although your appreciation of music could be spoilt if, all the time, you consciously concern yourself with assessments of metrical and rhythmic flexibility, metronome marks and the like, you should exercise, develop and enjoy your new-found awareness of them. At a concert or within earshot of a juke-box, when playing alone or singing in a choir, quickly guess at metronome speeds, identify time-signatures, notice the rhythmic cells within them and come to a personal conclusion about the artistry of the performers' rubato or rigidity as they add their own interpretative nuances to the inexact symbols of musical notation.

5

Pitch

5.1 Pitch dictation—if you need it

The aim in this chapter is first to consider pitching notes accurately, in tune, and incidentally some approximation to perfect pitch. Then we shall consider pitches sounded together in chords, creating an infinite variety of timbre and density. Finally we shall focus on some of the conventions of tonal harmony, progressing from one chord to another by singing and by playing.

Hitherto programmes of 'aural training' have laid heavy emphasis on identifying pitches and the letter-names of notes. This is required for recognizing intervals by name, writing down tunes from dictation, and identifying keys and modulations. The aim of this chapter is *not* specifically to develop this ability, useful as it may be to some, though the exercises and discussions may have incidental relevance to it. The skill, if you want to acquire it, is best developed on your own, as described in the Introduction. Play as much of a tuneful recording as you can confidently remember, repeat it as many times as you need, and then write it down. The printed score provides the unequivocally 'right' answer; you can adapt the difficulty of the task by shortening or lengthening the extract and playing it not twice but a dozen times, to suit yourself; there is no pressure on you to prove yourself against others or against the clock. This method will provide you with all the practice you need to learn to write down, from dictation, not only melodies (the solo violin part of a sonata, the treble line of a chorale) but also harmony (all four parts of a couple of bars of a string quartet 'Adagio', all four voices of a chorale). By the same method you can test your recognition of structure and modulations (the whole of a classical minuet in condensed sonata form, the development section of a piano sonata movement . . .).

Similar exercises can be invented to develop ability in identifying intervals. For example, sitting with eyes closed in front of a piano, play two notes, one with the index finger of each hand. Name the interval and confirm it by opening your eyes and looking at the keyboard. If you become too skilful at feeling how far apart your hands are, in front of you, turn round and play two notes behind your back!

Whether you value this skill or merely need it to pass an examination, such exercises will allow you to develop it in your own time, whenever and wherever you wish, rather than having to depend on the availability of a teacher to feed intervals to you.

5.2 Single pitches and intonation

Good intonation presents a constant challenge to performers of all but fixed-pitch instruments. Great care is taken to achieve it in instrumental and singing lessons and in ensemble rehearsals. Weaknesses are seized upon by critics. In fact it is often used as a yardstick for measuring musical ability and potential—to have a 'good ear' conventionally means to play or sing in tune. Yet this essential skill is often given a low priority in private practice, done alone and without reference to a fixed-pitch accompanying instrument.

The simplest aid to playing or singing in tune is an accompanist, and practice time can be greatly enhanced by allocating part of it to working with a pianist. Nor should the 'soloist' be apologetic about asking a friend to provide this service; far too many pianists restrict themselves to only that part of their repertoire to be played in piano recitals or concertos, omitting the musical riches and the technical demands and sensitivity of the duo partnership. Practising with an accompanist and simply remaining alert to intonation will itself improve it.

But there are in addition more concentrated ways of focusing on intonation. The following exercises offer a few suggestions; you will want to adapt and add to them in consultation with instrumental or singing teachers, and in the light of the technical requirements of the specific instrument which you play.

Exercises

First give yourself a note from a fixed pitch source such as piano, electronic keyboard, or tuning fork. Then sing or play: the note—the note above—the original note again. Check yourself against the fixed pitch. Extend this to wider intervals—C up to A♭ and back again, for example.

Second, play or sing up and down a scale very slowly indeed, in minims at crotchet = 40. Consciously sharpen each note and then drop back into tune again. Repeat the exercise, but this time flatten each note in the course of sounding it. (This illustrates a general principle, namely that you can develop an awareness of how to do something right by first exaggeratedly doing it wrong!)

Third, in a group of instrumentalists and/or singers, perform a chord, concentrating on getting it exactly in tune. Then very slightly alter each note of it in turn; hear the effect of a sharp major third, of a flat fifth, of an octave which buzzes with impurity.

Finally, sing or play a chord of G major, concentrating particularly on getting the B perfectly in tune. The B is, of course, functioning as the third of the chord. Then have someone add an F to the chord and analyse its effect on the B. Does it suddenly seem a touch flat? If so, it is because it now functions also as the leading note of C, and we have developed a tendency to tune leading notes rather sharp, encouraging them, as it were, to 'lead' up to the tonic note above.

5.3 Perfect pitch

Although very few people are blessed with 'perfect' or 'absolute' pitch, the ability to identify pitches without the aid of a given reference point, you can develop a fair approximation to it. Those who have it very acutely find that it can greatly enhance their musical appreciation. Pitches and keys can be associated with specific characteristics as vividly as most of us see colours or experience tastes. Then modulations take on a new significance, as keys not only depend for their effect on what has gone before but also are identifiable in their own right. G major is as clearly G major as red is red or Stilton is Stilton, and a modulation from it is, for some, as clearly perceived as a change to blue or to Roquefort.

This level of discrimination is rare, and some look on it as a mixed blessing, making it a painful experience to listen to a record playing slightly too fast or slow or to sing in an unaccompanied choir which has drifted slightly up or down. Furthermore, research shows that it must be acquired early. Few people develop it after the age of 11 or 12.

Although only the most accurate sense of perfect pitch will induce strong reactions to keys and key relationships, 'approximate pitch' is invaluable for singers and directors of musical ensembles. Unlike reliable 'perfect pitch' it can usually be acquired at any age, and simply by focusing your mind in particular ways upon everyday activities.

Some suggestions

First, before playing the first note of a practice session, guess at, and sing, an 'A'. String players should do this even before taking the instrument out of its case as merely handling it will make strings vibrate and give the game away.

Second, begin every choir practice with a unison 'A' or a D major chord, not prepared by a cue from a piano but plucked out of thin air. Initially the results may be cacophonous; after some weeks a measure of accord may develop.

Third, never pass a source of fixed pitch without singing an 'A'—or any other note if you prefer—and checking yourself. You may pass a piano in sitting room, practice room, lecture theatre or concert hall, twenty times a day. These are twenty opportunities to train yourself.

Finally, take note of the descriptions, in programmes, on record covers and in *Radio Times*, of the keys of works you are about to hear and hum your anticipation of the keynote just before the music begins.

5.4 Chordal characteristics

The exercises in section 5.3 are all designed for the individual performer, either alone or as a partner to one another. Equally important to composer as well as performer and listener is consideration of pitch in the denser musical context of a chord. For example, the notes of any given four-part chord can create markedly different musical effects depending on how they are distributed. Duplicate some or all of the notes in octave doublings, and the potential variety is further dramatically increased.

5.5 Exercises and discussion

First, in a group, four to eight, sing a chord of D major. Apart from agreeing that someone should sing the bottom note, D, to ensure that you produce D major in root position, choose your own notes. Have a conductor to encourage a confident ensemble—sing at least *mf*—and hold the sound for fifteen seconds. This will require all but the professional singers to take breaths: do so at will but not simultaneously, so that the sound remains sustained. Concentrate, both performers and listeners, not only on each person's contribution to the chord, singing the root, the third or the fifth, but also on the whole sound. Discuss, in threes at first, then as a larger group, what you experienced. Was the chord widely spaced or did many voices occupy one narrow part of the potential range? If the distribution was narrow, was it low or high? Was the density increased by doubled thirds—or were there, by chance, no thirds at all? Next repeat the performance but select a different note if you want to. In discussion, decide whether anyone did exercise this option. If so, who, and which note in the triad are they now singing? These questions are only examples. Any and every observation you make is valid provided it is true. Then sing one of the two versions while listening to the note your neighbour is singing. Repeat the performance but singing each other's notes.

Second, invite someone from the group to be a composer-conductor. Sing the chord indefinitely (breathing at will) and respond to gestures instructing some voices to drop out or return again, signalling dynamic changes or accents—or any other element which, after rehearsal, the conductor wishes to control. The conductor should avoid a haphazard performance. Imagine a sound first, and then use gestures which you think will produce it.

Subsequent discussion will be about the variety of effects obtainable from a single chord sung by a single medium, a choir. Particularly interesting will be to hear the conductor's reaction; for example, how far was an actual sound the one predicted in the conductor's imagination before gesturing to produce it?

5.6 Harmonic progression

A chord is musically almost meaningless in isolation. It takes on meaning only in a time continuum, coming from and/or going to another chord. Such progression is as much *melodic* as *harmonic*, as anyone learning western tonal harmony will know, and an excellent means of gaining insight into the melodic flow which creates harmonic progression is to sing it.

Exercises and discussion

Begin with a piano accompaniment, to give yourself confidence. Either a teacher can play, or you can accompany yourself by playing, slowly, the tonic and dominant chords of a key which suits you. Play it again and again: I-V-I-V-I-V-I—: I-V-I-V-I-V-I—. Then improvise a melody above the harmonic progression. Start as tentatively as you like, but gradually learn your own particular melody, which fits the harmony below. If you are working in a group, basses may like to sing the root position bass notes, while the counterpoint above can be in as many parts as there are additional singers. If you are working in a large class, a 'conductor' could be elected to choose a variety of changing densities—a solo quartet, perhaps, contrasting with the full choir—and to signal that only high voices/low voices should sing for a few bars. Some very alluring music can be created in this way—so beautiful that you might want to record it to enjoy again later.

As confidence increases, the accompanying piano can play more and more quietly until it fades out completely, at which point you could attempt to sing some progressions completely unaccompanied.

With the guidance only of an 'A' from the piano, and selecting notes at will as in section 5.5 (first exercise), sing a chord of D major with the addition of a minor seventh. Hold it for some seconds and then, on a signal from a conductor, resolve it to the chord of G major. Avoid breathing *between* the chords: this is a continuous harmonic progression, not two isolated musical events. Take particular note of the melodic movement you make. Those singing the bass D will probably leap to a G. F#, the leading note of G, will have an irresistible urge to rise. A may rise or fall by step, while C, the seventh, will certainly fall to B.

Experiencing harmonic progression from the inside, like this, is more revealing than any amount of verbal insistence in a textbook that leading notes rise and sevenths fall, for example.

Ex. 5.6a

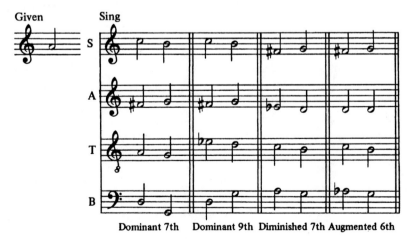

Dominant 7th   Dominant 9th   Diminished 7th   Augmented 6th

Additional single progressions which have sufficient inherent direction to be resolved intuitively include all the dominant additions—ninth, eleventh and thirteenth, 'six-four' chords, diminished sevenths—together with augmented sixths and Neapolitan sixths, which themselves have strongly 'dominant' qualities and will probably guide you to an intuitive resolution. (Observations on harmony are made in the light of this approach to the subject in George Pratt, *The Dynamics of Harmony: Principles and Practice*, OUP 1996; ISBN 0-19-879020-1.)

Ex. 5.6a makes the procedures clear.

5.7 Exercises

The experience of extemporizing harmony from the inside by singing it can, of course, be extended indefinitely.

First, given a piano 'A', sing $a^7 \to D^7 \to G$. (Lower case letters signify minor chords and upper case, major.) Take your time: spend five seconds on each chord and breathe *during* chords, not *between* them: these are progressions, and so must progress uninterrupted.

Second, take the cycle of fifths a stage further with $e^7 \to a^7 \to D^7 \to G$.

Third, exercise the option of colouring the minor chords with chromatic alterations—E^7 (the major version) $\to A^7 \to D^7 \to G$.

Fourth, reading a prepared chord sequence, sing an extended range of progressions. Any sequence will serve provided that it has a strongly directional quality, as for example Ex. 5.7a. Other progressions, in other keys, can be planned and written on a blackboard or read out to be jotted down on a scrap of paper.

Ex. 5.7a

$$G \longrightarrow D^7 \longrightarrow G \longrightarrow A^7 \longrightarrow D^6_4 \longrightarrow D^7 \longrightarrow G$$

or $\quad g \longrightarrow Eb \longrightarrow a^7 \longrightarrow D^7 \longrightarrow g \longrightarrow Ab^6 \longrightarrow D^6_4 \longrightarrow D^7 \quad :\|$

Fifth, reverting to a shorter sequence such as $G\text{—}D^7\text{—}G\text{—}D^7\text{—}G\text{—}a^7\text{—}D^7\text{—}G\|$, sing round it several times, as you did with the first exercise of 5.6, until you have established and memorized your own particular melody within it. At this point, you will be singing counterpoint in as many parts as there are singers in the group, unless any two hit upon the same melodic pattern. Next write down your melody. Then exchange manuscripts with your neighbour and read from it as the group sings the progression again. Commend or criticize the manuscript you have been given in a brief discussion.

Sixth, repeat the previous exercise, but this time feel free to decorate your melodic line with passing notes and rhythmic variations. Again, write it down, exchange it and perform your neighbour's composition. Then commend and criticize it in discussion.

The final challenge is to repeat the fifth exercise but, once your own melody is securely memorized, concentrate on and memorize what your neighbour is singing while continuing to sing your melody 'on autopilot'. Write down your neighbour's melody and ask him/her to check it.

All these exercises, simple enough at the beginning, can quickly become alarmingly difficult. There is no merit in failure; simplify the challenges instead, using a shorter chord sequence or limiting it to no more than tonic and dominant chords. It may take months of regular practice together to be able to extemporize on, and memorize, an ambitious chromatic chord sequence over eight bars. Four bars of two or three chords are more likely to encourage and reassure you with success.

5.8 Extending the exercises

So far, all the exercises in this chapter have been done by singing, an excellent way of getting inside harmonic progressions with your most ready-made and portable instrument. Instrumentalists should, though, be able to experience such progressions through their instruments (though they do so all too rarely), and the instrumental counterparts of the vocal exercises in sections 5.6 and 5.9 are explained later in section 10.4. Feel free to add to these vocal exercises the additional ones described in Chapter 10. As with most of the exercises in this book, they are intended to become part of a permanent repertoire, to be used, developed and extended indefinitely as your aural awareness increases. They are of very limited use if you simply try them a few times and then discard them.

5.9 Exercises

During the course of the twentieth century composers have expanded their harmonic and melodic vocabulary far beyond the triadic and dominant-driven style of the previous 300 years. This too can be experienced by extempore performance on instruments or by singing. Do not limit yourself to only one or the other.

First, build up a chord of perfect fourths by choosing, at will, either D, G, C or F after a cue from a piano 'A'. (Or perhaps, by now, you have approached near enough to perfect pitch to risk omitting the piano cue—see section 5.3!) Then play or sing a parallel progression in whole tones, as in Ex. 5.9a.

Ex. 5.9a

Second, devise further chords, for example using a note cluster, C, C♯ and D. Investigate the ways in which the timbre and density of the chord changes as you alter the distribution of the notes, or change the dynamic level and articulation from a fierce marcato forte to a softly sustained hum. Ex. 5.9b is very different from Exs. 5.9c and 5.9d. Sing and play them all.

Ex. 5.9b   Ex. 5.9c   Ex. 5.9d

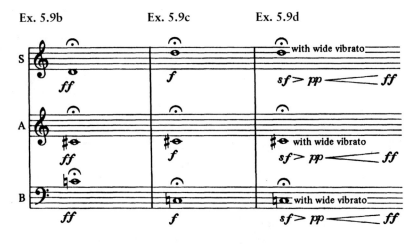

Third, create a chord based on fifths, as in Ex. 5.9e. Begin by singing parallel progressions up and down a major scale, as directed by a conductor. Then invent other ways of extemporizing with this new chord. For example, soprano and alto might move in contrary motion to tenor and bass. Again, have a conductor to guide you, perhaps one hand indicating the direction of movement, up or down, for soprano and alto and the other hand directing the remaining two voices. Finally, if you have access to a recording, listen to the opening twenty-two bars of the second movement, 'Adagio', of Bartok's Piano Concerto No. 2. This is entirely based on six-part fifth-chords, moving in contrary motion between the upper and lower groups of strings.

Ex. 5.9e

5.10 Do-it-yourself exercises

First, pick a sequence of three or four chords from a keyboard piece, preferably one you are learning if you are a keyboard player. Consider not only what they are (tonic, submediant first inversion, etc.), but also how they owe their character to the density and range of notes, to where they lie in the compass of the keyboard, to how loudly they are to be played, for what duration, in what rhythms.

Second, do the same exercise during a moment in an ensemble rehearsal—orchestra, band or choir—when the conductor rehearses a small fragment several times over. If you are not required to play, such moments are to be welcomed as invaluable opportunities to test your perceptions rather than being periods of boredom and inattention.

Finally, select a chord sequence in a recording—the first phrase of the vocal chorale which ends most Bach cantatas, say, or the opening two bars of a Schubert song. Play them enough times to be able to decide on an analysis of what the chords are and what elements in the way they are composed and performed give them their specific, perhaps unique, character.

6

Timbre

6.1 The perception and notation of timbre

Re-read section 2.4 to remind yourself of the meaning of 'timbre' or 'tone-colour', and its applications, ranging from the wholly obvious qualities which differentiate a string quartet from a brass band, the subtler difference between, say, the lowest and highest strings of a violin and, most subtle of all, the varieties of tonal character which a player can draw from any one single note.

At the crudest level, we are all blessed with 'perfect timbre', that is to say, we can identify and remember tone qualities sufficiently well to know at once whether we are listening to a quartet or a brass band without the need for some reference to remind ourselves of which is which every time we hear them. But our 'perfect timbre' stretches only so far; if you listen to a chord played on a Steinway piano this week, you could well not remember the timbre precisely enough to know that the same chord, next week, is being played on a Bechstein. So the aim of this chapter is to become more aware of timbral variety and to perceive and remember it more exactly as a composer choosing it, a listener appreciating it, and as a performer controlling it.

One way to achieve this is by notation, and a considerable proportion of the notation used at the earliest stages of composing and performing music is concerned with timbral definition. The National Curriculum requires pupils at Key Stage 1 to 'record their compositions using symbols, where appropriate', and many of these will be to act as reminders that at a particular point there will be a drum-beat, a scraping sound on a guiro, a spatter of 'rain' from a rainstick—all unpitched sounds, distinctive mainly for their timbral qualities. Paradoxically, in conventional western notation, timbre is only crudely notated. A score will generally specify instruments; some of what they play may be designated 'dolce' or 'con brio', 'sforzando' or 'senza vibrato', all terms with some timbral implications. But most of the timbral subtleties of actual performance are left to the discretion of players and conductors, and are often given rather low priority. You might think back to your own playing. How much of your last practice session was concerned with timbre? In the last orchestral rehearsal, did you think about your timbral quality? If so, what were you aiming for apart from such generalities as a 'good tone'. What *is* a 'good' tone? Do you always aim for the same *tone* at a particular moment in a piece—as you presumably aim for the same *pitches*?

The challenge of notating your own timbre is a very effective way of focusing your mind on this element.

6.2 Exercises and discussion

First, one person, a player of an orchestral instrument, should play a single note lasting for, say, five seconds. The rest of the group should then discuss what they have heard. Consider all the factors which contribute to timbre: the vigour and immediacy of the opening attack; the thickness of the sound and the constituent harmonics in it; the dynamic level (which influences the harmonic content—a strongly bowed violin note has more upper harmonics, creating a brighter sound, than a softly stroked note); whether the instrument is muted; where and how a string instrument is bowed or plucked; vibrato; stability or variability throughout the duration of the note; the immediacy with which it decays at the end.

Second, hear someone play a similar five-second note twice, making the performances as nearly identical as possible. Discuss how far this was achieved. It may well happen that you discern several differences, perhaps a rather alarming discovery in that most performers believe that they have a reasonable degree of control over what they are playing. Yet here are several inadvertent inconsistencies, not in a whole movement, or even in a phrase, but within a single five-second note, repeated once. The performer should not in fact be alarmed. It is your perception which is being heightened rather than your technique becoming unacceptably insecure!

Finally, it may equally well happen that there is disagreement about the timbral content of the two notes. This may be resolved or clarified by *notating* what you believe you hear. So, inventing whatever graphic marks will best serve your intentions, listen to another pair of supposedly identical five-second notes, and notate them accordingly. Next compare your notation first with that of your neighbour in the group. Discuss the two, deciding whether they are both accurate graphic representations of what you heard. Consider whether differences between them arise because you chose different graphic symbols or because you heard or analysed the sounds differently. Discuss and argue freely, and then expand the discussion to the whole group. Then do the whole notating exercise again in the light of any ideas for improving it you may have arrived at in your discussions.

Ex. 6.2a is a timbral notation of four performances of the opening of 'Narcissus', one of Britten's *Six Metamorphoses after Ovid* for solo oboe. Examine it (listen to one or more of the performances if you have access to the recordings) and decide how it differs, for better or for worse, from your own timbral notation. Adapt your own accordingly, if you wish.

This particular graphic notation is designed to pick up three features:

1. The immediacy of attack and decay, shown by arrows. The vigour of attack is shown by the angle of the arrow—vertical arrows imply strong tonguing and forceful breath; at 45°, attack and decay are moderate; horizontal arrows show notes growing from, and fading to, silence.
2. The nature of the performer's vibrato. The frequency of the waves shows the speed of vibrato; the amplitude refers to the width of vibrato.

3. The density of tone. Thin lines denote a thin tone; thick lines relate to rich tone with a complex harmonic spectrum.

Ex. 6.2a 'Narcissus', No. 5 from *Six Metamorphoses after Ovid*, Benjamin Britten (1913–76)

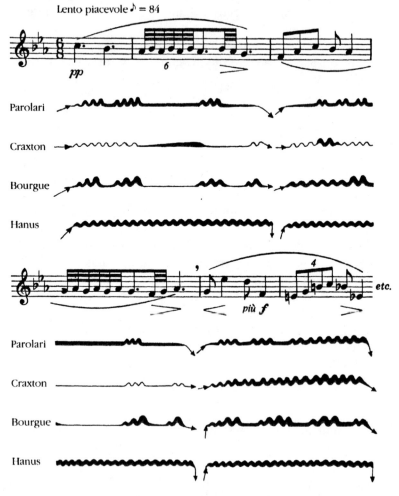

Notating even as few as these three timbral elements shows up some quite remarkable contrasts in interpretation. Egon Parolari's tone remains fairly constant throughout, while his vibrato tends to develop on held notes. Janet Craxton, on the other hand, varies her tone according to the dynamics. Two of the phrases begin so softly that there is no audible moment of attack. Maurice Bourgue applies vibrato to sustained notes even more than does Parolari. He attacks the third phrase quite explosively, while Viteslav Hanus ends each phrase very abruptly and, for him, vibrato appears to be a constant tremor rather than an expressive musical device.

The analysis can go further, of course. But two important points of a more general nature arise from the exercise. First, that we are not trying to invent a universally accepted notation of timbre. You are simply equipping yourself with an aid to timbral analysis, so none of your notation is 'right' or 'wrong'. If it serves you adequately as a means of focusing attention on timbral details and recording them, it is perfectly satisfactory.

Second, it is quite remarkable that *not one* of the timbral interpretative details of the four performances in Ex. 6.2a is represented in conventional notation. Although the performances are very different, none is necessarily better nor more correct than the others as far as the composer's written instructions are concerned. It is the unwritten interpretative details, including timbre, which may well make one aesthetically more pleasing than the other.

If there is an oboist in your group, you could hear a performance of Ex. 6.2a in an approximation to all four versions.

6.3 Do-it-yourself exercises

First, listen at home or in a record library to two different recordings of the same work, to compare their timbral characteristics. Best at this stage are unaccompanied pieces for a single-line instrument. Suggestions include:

1. *Syrinx* by Debussy (solo flute) [CLAV 50704 and RCA 74321 37731-2];
2. *Six Metamorphoses after Ovid* by Britten (solo oboe) [HYPE CDA 66776 and PHIL 434 076-2];
3. 'L'Abîme des oiseaux', from *Quartet for the End of Time* by Messiaen (solo clarinet) [DG 423 247-2 and COLL 1393-2];

4. The opening of *The Rite of Spring* by Stravinsky (solo bassoon) [EMI CDC7 49636 and EMI CD-EMX 2188];
5. 'Prologue', from *Serenade for Tenor, Horn and Strings* by Britten (solo horn) [PEAR GEMMCD 9177 and EMIN CD-EMX 2247];
6. Many movements of the *Sonatas and Partitas for Violin Alone* by Bach [HYPE CDD 22009 and PHIL 438 736-2];
7. Most movements of the *Six Suites for Solo 'Cello* by Bach [RCA RD 70950 and DG 449 711-2];
8. Cadenzas to concertos on record.

If these are not available, limit yourself at least to other solo instruments such as piano, harpsichord or harp. As soon as two or more instruments combine, the timbral range becomes very much wider, until it reaches the extreme complexity of a full romantic symphony orchestra. Limit yourself, too, to a manageable span of music. It might be only a few seconds if you want to remember every detail. Create a graphic score of the two performances, notating only their timbral qualities, not pitches, rhythms, or any other 'elements' except in so far as these affect the timbre—a *forte* generating a bright or aggressive tone, a *legato* inhibiting marked attack and decay on the notes in a slurred phrase.

Second, consider which of the two performances you prefer. Perhaps each has attractive timbral characteristics which would enhance the other. Perhaps neither has quite the character you would give it if you were the performer. So *think* through the performance in your memory (one good reason for selecting a short passage from a piece) and ensure that this imagined performance has all the timbral attributes you think it requires.

Third, too much concentration on repeated listenings to a small fragment of music can be a disheartening experience. Although it is a valuable exercise to observe every minute detail, the broader view of the whole work is also essential. Listen, therefore, to a performance of a whole work, preferably written for your own instrument or voice. Then write a critique of the performer's timbral resources—the qualities of sound, the range of tone colours, the technical devices used to achieve them such as vibrato, hard tonguing, bowing 'sul ponticello', dynamic extremes. . . . Particularly fruitful sources of contrasted performances are those of earlier music on 'authentic' instruments. Here relevant factors in analysing timbre will include structure and materials—the shorter lighter bow of a baroque violin and the gut strings on which it plays; the veiled sound of cross-fingered notes on a flute and the tone quality of box-wood rather than metal.

Finally, the hardest task of all is to hear subtleties of timbre not from recordings or live performance but simply in your imagination. Prepare to play a recording of a simple sound—the first chord of a piano sonata or the opening few notes of one of the single-line pieces suggested in the first exercise would serve very well. Imagine the sound you are about to hear, in as much detail as possible—not a generalized woodwind note, say, but a modern oboe, at such-and-such a level in its range, even perhaps being played by a particular artist whom you admire. Then play the recording and see how nearly you hit upon the actual sound. This can be extended as far as you like. For example, you may take a much more complex sound such as the first chord of a full orchestral tutti or a moment from an unfamiliar, perhaps contemporary, piece for chamber ensemble. Another way of developing the exercise is to silently read a melody—hymn tune or Beatles song—imagining it to be played on a particular instrument. Try 'Yellow Submarine' for viola or 'Rock of Ages' on the alto saxophone. (This skill of hearing silently, 'imaging', is taken further in Chapter 9.)

6.4 Timbre for performers

So far, we have considered timbre mainly from the point of view of composers who have to imagine it accurately and notate their music accordingly, and of listeners who respond to it with greater or lesser degrees of perception. The gap between composer and listener is bridged by the performer, so the following exercises and discussions are intended to heighten your awareness of the timbral qualities already present in your playing, and to expand the range of those qualities. Simply being aware of what tonal resources you have at your disposal will help you to use them tastefully and subtly, while the more you find you have, the greater your range of choice as you develop your own personal interpretation of a piece of music.

6.5 Exercises and discussion

Extend the first exercise in section 6.2 from playing a single note to playing an extended phrase. Younger players can be challenged to play on electronic keyboards but, at more advanced levels, you will probably be best served by someone playing an orchestral wind or string instrument. While not suggesting that an acoustic or electronic piano, say, presents no timbral challenges, the direct physical contact of breath or bow, coupled with the demands of fingering, make it harder to sustain absolute consistency between two performances—and the aim is to have something imperfect enough to give rise to discussion. Indeed you may need to ask your performer to build in subtle variations to provide something with which to develop a lively discussion. However, it is remarkably difficult to play a single octave scale of C major on the piano twice without there being some detectable difference between the first and second playings.

In the ensuing discussion, be as precise as possible. It is not enough simply to declare that the performances differed. You will need to identify exactly where and how: the second note had more vibrato; the climax of the phrase was louder and brighter in tone; the last note faded away more markedly. If recording equipment is available (a cassette recorder with a built-in microphone is better than nothing) it is worth recording the two performances, if only as a means of resolving arguments later.

Next, the player, still sitting or standing in front of the rest of the group, should attempt to play the phrase with as little timbral variation as possible. This boring performance will need very precise placing, angle and distribution of the bow, and up-strokes and down-strokes will have to be indistinguishable from each other—or breath will have to be controlled with absolute evenness, and no one note be tongued more or less forcefully than the rest. The audience should criticize errors or commend success.

78

The player should then play the same phrase but with planned variations. One motif may be 'sul ponticello', another with bow flat and a wide vibrato—or a vigorous tongue and changed embouchure may make half a bar stand out from the rest. Again, the audience should comment, identifying the place, nature and degree of the timbral variations.

Finally, revert to the opening of this exercise to see if the player can perform, and listeners can confirm, two performances which are identical. If they are not, the exercise has not failed. The primary aim is to be aware of timbral qualities. Controlling them is an ongoing challenge, never wholly to be resolved in a lifetime by a truly critical artist.

6.6 Further exercises

Invent further exercises of your own after discussion. The following are ideas which can be developed.

First, with two players of the same instrument having mastered the notes of a given phrase,

X plays it: Y imitates it: the audience approves or criticizes.

Y plays it: X imitates it: the audience approves or criticizes.

X + Y discuss their performances and, with the audience also making suggestions, agree on a preferred interpretation.

X plays it: Y imitates it: the audience comments.

Y plays it: X imitates it: the audience comments.

Imitation of this kind plays a very important part in the teaching of music of some cultures. A student of sitar, learning from a master of the instrument, will spend many years watching, listening and imitating. Perhaps the ability to absorb music in this way is dulled for western musicians, whose notational system is relatively sophisticated. Those who play so much by eye have a great deal to learn from those who play more or less exclusively by ear.

Second, a performer plays an extended phrase or two and, with the help of the audience, identifies two separate notes or motifs which require the same timbral interpretation. They are both isolated and practised, ensuring that bow angles and speeds or embouchure and tonguings are consistent, meeting the critical demands of the audience. Then the phrase is played complete and its successful evolution confirmed.

Finally, a performer has available two or more instruments or bows, or head-joints with contrasting reeds, and plays a short phrase on each instrument in turn, behind the back of the audience. Then the performance is repeated but not necessarily with the instruments in the same order. The audience has to identify which performance was on the Stradivarius and which on the plywood violin—which on the wooden flute and which on the silver one.

6.7 Extending timbre

Traditionally most performance requires instruments to be used in conventional ways, benefiting from the very qualities for which they have been developed. Of course developments, in turn, are usually in response to the evolving demands of music. So the structure and materials of the baroque violin and bow have been superseded by others in order that the instrument can generate the power required of it in a romantic symphony orchestra and, equally, the later instrument is increasingly seen as inadequate for the authentic performance of earlier music.

Sometimes, though, composers will search for completely new timbral qualities from instruments, often not derived from the sounds they have been specifically developed to produce. So while bow-makers' efforts have always been to produce the best possible device for stroking strings with horse-hair, Haydn required his violinists to play with the wood, 'col legno' (in Symphony No. 67 [LOND 448 531-2]). More recently, composers have increasingly exploited unusual sounds. Examples include Béla Bartók's invention of the pizzicato which snaps down on to the fingerboard, for which he devised the symbol ♦ (String Quartet No. 4, Sz 91, 1928 [ASV CDDCS 301]), John Cage's complex preparation of a grand piano by inserting wedges and screws at very precisely defined points between certain strings ('Sonatas and Interludes', 1946–8 [MUSI MACD-937]) and William Brooks's writing for voices with reinforced harmonics so that each singer produces two notes at once ('Madrigals', recorded in 1982). There are innumerable additional examples.

One feature of this process is that the timbral spectrum of composers, performers and listeners alike is constantly being expanded, while imaginations flourish and perceptions deepen— developments in which we can share and through which our own awareness can be extended.

6.8 Exercises and discussion

First, discover an unconventional sound using all or part of your instrument. Ideas might include bowing beyond the bridge or blowing across the tube of a flute with the head-joint removed. The possibilities are endless, and should be limited only by any risk of damaging your instrument—the extended timbral spectrum of a 'cello splintering is not recommended! Then notate the sound. Discuss with your neighbour the accuracy of the relationship between sound and notation.

Second, notate a sound which you imagine can be made on your instrument but which you have not yet performed. Then perform it and again discuss the sound and its notation with a neighbour. Refine your notation if new ideas have occurred to you.

Third, explore further the timbral potential of your instrument or voice and then repeat the first two exercises to discover whether you have refined your analysis and notation of unconventional sounds.

Fourth, notate a sound for your neighbour's instrument or voice and assess, when it is performed, how accurately you had imagined it and communicated your intentions by notation.

Fifth, working in groups of four, write a quartet for yourself and your three neighbours lasting for, say, sixteen bars or about forty seconds. This will require the kind of exploring, controlling and notating of sounds which is now common practice in composition at school, college and university, but using extended instrumental/vocal sounds rather than the conventional ones for which instruments are primarily designed.

Perform the quartet(s), recording them if possible, and then discuss the rationale behind the selection of sounds and their notation. Amend compositions and notations at will and end with a further performance.

Finally, the previous exercise can be amended to allow the creation of an extempore piece, of particular value to composers requiring experience in combining instrumental tone qualities at any level of complexity up to full orchestration. A maximum of eight performers, in turn, play their own lines, composed at the start of the previous exercise and a composer/conductor attempts to memorize each range of timbres and rhythms. Then the conductor selects, with conventional hand gestures or by calling out names or numbers, a range of the available musical material, blending, contrasting, stopping and starting any or all of the eight 'parts' at will. Subsequent discussion should focus on such issues as:

1. What principles guided the conductor's selection of players?
2. How far did the conductor accurately predict the result and how much artistic control was really being exercised?
3. What interactions worked best or worst and why?

6.9 Applying timbral awareness

Such experiments and exercises as these can be taken very seriously indeed, or can lead to considerable mirth. Either is wholly acceptable, so long as you remain constantly aware of the purposes behind the activities. Composers need the highest possible level of ability in imagining timbral qualities accurately and in communicating them by clearly intelligible notation, and performers need a similar level of awareness of the whole timbral spectrum, both to read a composer's intentions and to perform them wholeheartedly: the whole process is pointless if listeners are not sensitive to the efforts of composers and performers alike.

So you should take your timbral awareness, enhanced by these exercises and any others you may devise, into every musical activity from its first conception, through its realization to its final appreciation.

6.10 Do-it-yourself exercises

First, make a 'timbral score' of some of your own playing, using any graphic notation which will serve your purposes.

Second, test the timbral consistency of your playing, either by self-criticism or by inviting a friend to listen to a few minutes of your private practice.

Third, listen for exceptional timbres, common enough in much *avant garde* music but present, too, to create the sound which characterizes and identifies a new pop group or which differentiates one player or one orchestra from another. Write a brief descriptive summary of what you have heard.

Fourth, search among the scores in the music library (institutional or municipal) for examples of composers conceiving and notating unconventional sounds. If records are available, listen to some to expand your timbral repertoire.

Finally, several available books are concerned with both the production and the notation of unconventional sounds. Look for any of the following in your libraries.

Kurt Stone, *Music Notation in the Twentieth Century: A Practical Guidebook*, New York, W. W. Norton, 1980.
Phillip Rehfeldt, *New Directions for Clarinet*, University of California Press, 1977.
Thomas Howell, *The Avant-garde Flute: A Handbook for Composers and Flutists*, University of California Press, 1974.
Bruno Bartolozzi, *New Sounds for Woodwind* (2nd edn), Oxford University Press, 1982.

7

Criticism

7.1 Exercising critical judgement

Most of the exercises in the three previous chapters have been
concerned with identifying the presence of particular musical
features but not necessarily deciding whether their presence is
desirable. The process has been one of observation rather than
exercising critical judgement. In the timbral analysis of six bars
of Britten's 'Narcissus' (Ex. 6.2a) there proved to be a remarkable number of differences between the four performances. Yet
we have studiously avoided declaring that one performance was
'better' than the others, or even that the use of a single accent,
any one moment of vibrato, a specific gradient of dynamic
change, was preferable to the other performers' interpretations.
The exercises in section 3.8, for example, demanded a level of
judgement beyond simple observation, to decide whether particular musical events created 'tension' or 'release'. But still there
was no call for critical judgement: tension is not necessarily
preferable to release, or vice versa.

The primary aim, in this chapter, is to apply critical judgement
to our observations, to add a further stage to the process of
developing our perceptions to the highest level we can. First,
observe the effectors—what happens in the music. Then determine the effects—the creation of tension or release. Finally, criticize the effects—how far they are desirable.

This is not intended to develop into a full-blown study of the aesthetics of music (excellently introduced by the article on this subject by F. E. Sparshott in *The New Grove Dictionary of Music*, Macmillan, London, 1980). Rather, we shall examine various kinds and levels of criticism, try out the most useful ones in exercises and discussion and finally, and most importantly, feed any new awareness and experience back into everyday musical activity.

7.2 The 'music critic'

A common outlet for what purports to be 'criticism' of compositions and performances is through daily newspapers and specialist music journals. It is worth examining some of these writings, to decide whether their techniques have anything to teach us.

1. At their most superficial, they consist of little more than announcements that events have taken place.
2. At the next level, descriptions of performances and compositions may use words which imply critical evaluation but lack any supporting reasons for the judgement. A critic writing that a performance was 'beautiful' or 'sensitive' describes only a personal reaction which may be based on completely inaccurate premises or a wholly idiosyncratic view of how the music should be played.
3. A critic achieves a more credible level of criticism when supporting it with clear implications of what criteria the judgement is based on.
4. The highest level of criticism lays down clearly what are the criteria for judgement, measures the performance/composition against them, and refers explicitly to any influencing factors outside the music itself.

Clearly it is unrealistic to expect this deepest level of criticism in much of what we read. The junior football correspondent of the local weekly paper is adequately fulfilling a limited aim by announcing that Miss Smith sang some songs at a concert in the village hall, accompanied at the pianoforte by Mr Jones—level 1 above.

Adding that Miss Smith was in fine voice and sang expressively to a large and enthusiastic audience, while Mr Jones's playing was pleasing, would demonstrate a certain level of personal reaction from the critic, and from the audience too—level 2 above.

A more sophisticated review might add that Miss Smith also varied her tone reflecting the emotion and period of the various songs while Mr Jones's playing was very 'authentic'. Then the critic's approval would be based on widely accepted criteria, even though they were more implicit than explicit: the reader must assume that variation of tone quality and 'authenticity' (whatever that may be) are good things—level 3 above.

Although the junior football correspondent is unlikely to achieve criticism at level 4, it must be the constant aim of every composer and performer judging their own work, and of every listener responding to it. Here Miss Smith's songs would need listing and the individual requirements assessed. This assessment itself needs justification. An early-nineteenth-century German Lied describing sorrow at lovers' parting, written for a known singer reported to have a rich contralto voice, exploring the lowest part of the range, at a slow metronome marking and with extended phrases and held notes above dense chromatic chords—this spells out at least some of the treatment the song requires, absolutely, if the singer is to be true to the composer's intentions. Mr Jones's 'authenticity' meanwhile might extend to the use of a Viennese pianoforte made by André Stein in 1815, for which he has had specialist training in a conservatoire 'Early Music' performance course. Both performers would be using the most reliable 'Urtext' (original text) edition and would have indicated to the audience, on programme notes or in spoken introduction, any information about the circumstances of the song's composition which should influence performance and appreciation of it.

Yet even this is only part of musical criticism as it omits the personal and intuitive response which endows a performance with an individual and unique quality while still keeping it within the limits of fidelity to the composer. Conventional notation retains a degree of imprecision which allows freedom to performers. Indeed, the absence of such freedom detracts from the emotional and aesthetic appeal of a performance: a recording, however faithful it may be to the composer's intentions, never changes and so can never explore the range of legitimate variations. The soprano's timbre through a particular moment of exultation or melancholy will always be the same at every hearing; we can no longer share the trumpeter's anxiety about an extremely high note nor his relief at hitting it accurately; the unexpectedness of an abrupt modulation is dulled after repeated hearing. The same is true of that part of electro-acoustic music in which the composer freezes sound in the act of composition, and 'performance' consists of playing back a tape or music stored in the RAM of a computer.

So beware of allowing criticism to be so clinical and objective that it ignores the unique contribution of the human spirit.

7.3 Functions of criticism

For our purposes, then, criticism is essential in all three musical activities, composing, performing, and actively listening. Its functions are

1. to analyse the elements of which a given span of music is made;
2. to explore the ways in which these elements act alone, and interact with each other;
3. to synthesize these actions and interactions into musical effects—at their simplest, describable as 'tension' and 'release';
4. to establish whether these effects are desirable or not, measured against historical facts and stylistic conventions;
5. to recognize and compensate for factors which may make our judgement unreliable.

7.4 Criteria for judgement

The first three functions of criticism are the subjects of Chapters 2 and 3. Read through these chapters again, thinking also of the

87

experiences you will have gained when doing the exercises and discussing them with others.

The fourth function, requiring a prior knowledge of historical facts and stylistic conventions, demonstrates very clearly that all aspects of the study of music are interrelated. A scholar may investigate eighteenth-century theorists' writings to decide how a baroque trill should be played. So performers depend on such research in order to decide how to interpret baroque music. But equally, the scholar's research is pointless until it is played by performers and experienced by listeners.

Biographical and sociological information too can often be crucial to composition and performance, even though at first sight it appears to be divorced from music. Suppose, for example, you are a soprano, due to prepare for performance the aria 'Rejoice greatly' from Handel's *Messiah*. To arrive at an interpretation which makes at least an honest effort to express Handel's intentions, you would be helped by all the following information—and more.

1. Handel's youthful travels in Italy gave him first-hand experience of Italian opera upon which he based his career in London.
2. His success as a composer of Italian opera in London had waned by 1741 as he faced commercial competition, religious opposition and changing public fashions.
3. He wrote 'Rejoice greatly' originally in triplet quavers (in $\frac{12}{8}$ time) but rewrote it with semiquavers ($\frac{4}{4}$ time) for a specific operatic soprano, Giulia Frasi.
4. She was described as having 'a sweet clear voice, and a smooth and chaste style of singing [and] she pronounced our language in singing with a more distinct articulation' than did many native English singers.

Thus biographical details about Handel, fragments of economic and social history, of the textual evolution of the score of *Messiah* and of a contemporary description of a particular performer's voice all play a part in determining that 'Rejoice greatly' should be sung in a manner not far removed from that of baroque opera, with clarity, sweetness, clear diction and responding to the challenges of virtuoso semiquavers. If this information were universally known, we might be spared many inappropriate castings for this soprano role!

The fifth function of criticism, the factors which may impair our judgement, are too many to list inclusively. Some examples are

- *Our familiarity with a work or a style.* As we hear a work for the first time, our attitudes towards it and what we actually perceive of it will be different from our attitudes and perceptions when the work has become more familiar. Furthermore, if we already know the composer's style, we will have certain expectations even if we are hearing the specific work for the first time. (Exercise and discussion: identify a piece known to some of the group but not to all. An effective choice might be a piece which one member of the group has learned fairly thoroughly. Play it once, and compare your critical reactions to it. Those familiar with it will probably have fairly strong opinions about its performance. The rest may be more nearly indifferent.)
- *Knowledge of historical factors affecting the quality of the sound.* You may, for example, be disappointed by the tone quality of a baroque 'cello playing a Bach 'Cello Suite simply because you have been taught to appreciate the sound and bowing techniques of a modern instrument.
- *Knowledge of instrumental techniques.* If you can play an instrument your response to it may well be more critical, or more forgiving, than if you know it solely as a listener.
- *Knowledge of a specific performer's style.* Taken to extremes, this can produce the kind of uncritical adulation and hero-worship afforded to pop stars, opera singers and 'maestro' conductors. (Exercise and discussion: hear a recording of an unfamiliar piece. Write a brief critique of it. Then pool your knowledge about it, its historical context, its composer, the performers, their instruments—the kind of information offered by some detailed record sleeve notes. Then hear it again and decide whether you would want to modify your initial critique in the light of your enhanced understanding.)

- *Cueing.* The views of other people colour our own opinions.
- *Mood.* We can respond to music with tremendous enthusiasm on one occasion and find it leaves us cold on another. Indeed, we often select recreational listening to suit our mood, while advertisers, for example, constantly affect our mood by their selection of music. (Exercise and discussion: video-record some television advertisements. Watch them through, considering particularly the character and style of the music accompanying them. Then select and record on cassette some alternative music, making it as inappropriate as possible. Play back simultaneously the video picture without sound and your chosen taped music. The effects are very striking indeed—and often quite hilarious.)
- *The context of the performance.* A series of bad performances will make a better one seem disproportionately good—a phenomenon of which examiners and adjudicators have to beware.

7.5 Exercise and discussion

The whole critical process can now be tried. One person in the group should give a performance of a short piece lasting, say, two minutes. Then everyone, performer and listeners alike, should write a criticism of the performance. Keep in mind a check-list of bases for your judgement:

1. What musical 'elements' does the music particularly depend on?
2. How far are they observed and how committedly are they expressed by the performer?
3. Do they generate the tensions and releases of which they are potentially capable?
4. As you form your opinions, what information may you need—historical facts, understanding of the composer's style and period, awareness of instrumental or vocal techniques, knowledge of any particular circumstances surrounding the composition of the piece?
5. Are there any external factors which might be temporarily clouding your judgement?

When your 'criticisms' are written, share your views, at first with a neighbour, then in the larger group. Remember, at this point, that 'criticism' does not simply consist of adverse comment. Your critical judgement should make you as ready to commend as to censure.

In the light of this discussion, the performance should then be repeated. Then repeat the written critique. The performance itself may well be different, profiting from the ideas thrown up in discussion. Your critical comments, at least, will be more expansive as you share or refute the whole range of judgements made after the first performance.

The final discussion should attempt, first, to produce a measure of agreement about the performance based on well-argued views, studiously avoiding superficial reactions which cannot be supported by evidence—not 'I just like it' but 'I like it *because* . . .', and second, to propose practical measures to improve the performance at every level from mechanical techniques like changing a fingering, through larger-scale management of phrasing, articulation, dynamics and speed, to re-interpretation based on a sensitivity to style and on historical information which may be at several removes from the details of the piece.

7.6 Do-it-yourself exercises

The material in this chapter is mainly concerned with attitudes, and processes which you will do alone. By all means engage in group criticism during the interval of a concert or after hearing a recording together. But the critical perceptions are particularly important to you when you are alone, composing or practising. Indeed, you can increase the benefit of practice enormously just by applying to it a critical ear and avoiding practising on 'auto-pilot'.

First, have a pencil and paper beside you while you practise for half-an-hour. Jot down critical comments (positive commendations as well as negative censure) while you work. Then criticize your criticism: assess your assessment. On what criteria is it based? How far is it reasoned and analytical? How far emotional? How far simply a gut-reaction?

Second, repeat the exercise, but with a friend to listen, observe, and write comments about your practice. After, say, fifteen minutes, reverse roles—you sit jotting down a critique while your partner gets on with a quarter of an hour of intensive practice.

Third, compare two recordings of a piece of music. Use no more than a movement—less if you prefer—so that the time-span does not become too daunting and you revert to generalizations. For every critical decision which you make, ensure you have supporting reasons: not 'I thought the tone was good'; perhaps 'I thought the tone was good because it seemed even and under control'; but better 'I thought the tone was good because it was appropriate (how?) to the demands of the piece (namely?)'.

Finally, listen to a manageable piece of music—a movement or less. Write two criticisms of it, creating two contrasting arguments, one in favour, one against. A good starting-point would be a piece of baroque music played either on original instrument(s) *or* on their modern equivalent. Argue, for example, that the 'original instrument' performance produced a particular timbre, encouraged a particular approach to pitch, rhythms, articulations, dynamic range, speed, which faithfully reflected the composer's intentions. Then argue for the greater tonal and dynamic range and the increased density which are available on modern instruments and which the composer may have preferred if they had been available.

It does not matter which of these views you hold personally. The exercise is intended not only to focus your attention on the criteria of musical criticism, but also to generate tolerance, if not acceptance, of a variety of views. Dogmatic attitudes lead to unreliable critical judgements.

8

Structure

8.1 'Structure' and 'form'

So far we have examined musical events largely independently of each other—one element, then the next. But as isolated moments of sound are not, in themselves, music, so too it can be misleading to examine isolated layers of musical quality—pitch without reference to timbre, rhythm without reference to dynamics.

The aim of this chapter is to identify some of these relationships in music. They are both simultaneous—the elements (pitch, rhythm, articulation, phrasing, dynamics, timbre) of a melody related to an accompanying texture, for example—and consecutive, that is the repetition or alteration of elements during the course of a piece.

In notated art music, these structural relationships are often very complex, and develop over a long time-span. Folk music, handed down by aural tradition, has simpler structures. Because of the complexity of art music, this kind of structural analysis is normally carried out with scores and the production of tabular listings, diagrams, skeleton outlines of deeper and deeper layers of perception and, increasingly nowadays, computer graphics. All these, wholly valid though they are, tend to be visual rather than aural processes. Indeed, the pace of the actual music is so retarded in such processes that the ear can hardly cling on to the sense of a continuum of sound. So this chapter is *not* concerned with traditional, largely visual, analysis of musical structures.

That is very well introduced in *The New Grove Dictionary* article, 'Analysis', by Ian Bent.

Nor is this a chapter about *form*. Within the National Curriculum the terms *form* and *structure* have become rather confused. The requirements of Key Stage 3 include that 'pupils should be taught to listen with understanding and identify the development of musical ideas, investigating, internalising and discriminating within and between the musical elements of: . . . structure—forms based on single ideas, *eg riff*; forms based on alternating ideas, *eg rondo, ternary*, forms based on developmental ideas, *eg variation, improvisation.*' For the purposes of our understanding in this chapter at least, most of these are examples of *forms*, of the moulds into which composers pour their music. They include the tonal scheme of classical sonata movements or the strophic shape of a romantic song. *Structure* refers to the organization of all the musical elements *within* forms. It is those aspects which are wholly matters of the composer's choice—where, how and in what proportions to modulate within a sonata-form movement; whether or not to vary the texture, instrumentation, figuration or harmony from one verse of a strophic song text to the next. There must be tens of thousands of movements in sonata *form*: that each one is different is due to the way in which composers *structure* them, from the briefest detail to the largest overall scale.

Sometimes structure and form coincide; many a second-rate eighteenth-century minuet consists of exactly sixteen bars to the dominant at a double bar followed, after eight new bars, by the original sixteen again with one predictable alteration to remain in the tonic. First-rate minuets, on the other hand, may well diverge from such conventional formalized proportions, not to the point of total imbalance but sufficiently to be admired for their originality.

Exercise and discussion

Spend five minutes compiling a list of ways in which musical elements can be manipulated structurally at the kind of level that can be heard and understood at an early stage of getting to know a piece of music. For example, any musical event can be *repeated*. Then discuss your list with a neighbour, expand it accordingly, and finally pool all your suggestions. Do not read on! Some possible contributions to such a list are given below.

8.2 Manipulations

You may conclude that there are six ways of handling a musical phenomenon. It can be *repeated*, *sustained*, *altered* by expansion or contraction, *inverted*, *reversed*—or simply *abandoned*.

Exercises and discussion

A very flexible exercise which can be done to various levels of detail and sophistication is to listen to any couple of minutes or so of a slow piece of music. Then, while listening two or three more times, begin drawing a 'structural map' of what you hear. Gradually fill in more detail until, after about four hearings, you have before you a 'score' of all the structural blocks—sections unified by a common scoring; sections contrasting in some way—in timbre perhaps, or in dynamics; repetitions and near-repetitions of motif or melody. Try something as well known as the slow movement of Dvořák's Symphony No. 9, 'From the New World' [Decca 448 245-2]. At a first hearing you could probably identify the four bars of brass chords, a two-bar breath of strings, before the familiar cor anglais melody. Second and third hearings might reveal that the melody itself is clearly divisible into one two-bar motif answered by another, before another repeated motif over suspended harmonies. Back then to the original melody, but off into a different direction at the end. And then, a clarinet echo of the ending, twice, unwinding the initial pace to half-speed. All of this is *structure*, the composer's shaping of the material he has created.

Almost any section of music slow enough for the ear and the brain to take in its flow can be analysed structurally like this. But, as you gain experience, you can deepen the level of analysis, particularly by referring to the musical elements we have identified earlier (Chapter 2).

For such an exercise, listen several times to the first seventeen bars of Mozart's Clarinet Quintet (K581) [HYPE CDA 66199]. Do *not* on any account look at a score. (If you are working alone, without a tutor to start and stop a recording at the right moment, you need to know only that the clarinet ends its second two-bar rising arpeggio and falling arabesque on the first beat of bar 17.) Note that the movement is in $\frac{2}{2}$ time, beginning with a bar of two minims.

Consider each element in relation to the ways in which it may be handled structurally. After discussion and the pooling of ideas, you may have reached some conclusions such as the following list.

1. A more or less constant *metre* is *sustained* throughout.
2. The *rhythmic* intensity is *altered* by being contracted over eight bars—minims → crotchets → quavers (off-beat accompanying chords) → semiquavers (as the clarinet plunges down half-way through and at the end). Rhythmically the seventeen bars fall into two *repeated* nine-bar sentences, overlapping so that the first sentence ends (the resolution of the clarinet arabesques) as the second begins (the string minims).
3. *Pitch* outlines also fall into two *repeated* sections, though there are subtle *alterations* both in melodic outline and in harmonic progression. The pitch of the second clarinet entry is *repeated* in its outline shape but *altered*, expanding upwards to the next step in the arpeggio. After some (actually seven) bars of downward movement from first violin, the clarinet *inverts* this direction in a single bar before falling again through semiquaver arabesques.
4. The *texture* too is *repeated* almost exactly: uniformly rhythmical chords → melody above repeated off-beat quavers → clarinet solo rising, and then falling above a *sfz* chord. For one bar only, the second sentence differs in texture from the first. Will concentrated listening reveal this minute structural development?
5. *Timbre* is precisely the same from one section to the other except in so far as the tone of the clarinet is brighter the second time simply because its *compass* is *altered* (higher).

6. There is a fascinating range of *density*: although it, too, is repeated from one eight-bars-plus-one-beat to the next, the opening chord of each section is remarkably conceived and spaced, with two major thirds increasing the density, but with a two-octave space between them creating a compensating rarity. *Articulations*, too, influence the density as lower strings *expand* the vitality of the accompaniment by *abandoning* a homophonic role and *contracting* note-values to off-beat quavers.

7. *Dynamic* structure will depend to some extent on the interpretation of the five performers of your recording, but there should certainly be a sense of calm piano at the start, interrupted by a *sfp* attack from inner strings below the arabesques. Dynamics, too, are *repeated*—the '9 + 9 = 17' structure is reinforced by every element.

8. The rhythmic *alteration-through-contraction* at the beginning carries with it an *alteration* in harmonic *pace*—not only do note-values halve (in bar 3) but also harmonies change twice as frequently. From the following bar, though, the *pace* of harmonic change reverts to *sustained* minims and, below the clarinet, *expands* to semibreves—one harmony to a bar. So *harmonic pace* is at variance with *rhythmic pace*.

It is quite unlikely that all these comments will emerge from three or four hearings and discussion; moreover, should you find others, they will be no less valid than these. If, though, you hit on a few, or any, of them, you will be recognizing the interrelationships of musical elements, in both the vertical structure of simultaneous events, and the horizontal structure of succeeding events through a span of time. The crotchets of bar 3 make their impact only because they contrast with the first two bars of minims.

A final stage in this exercise and discussion is to create a 'score' of these musical events. Draw bar-lines to create seventeen bars, either on paper if you are working individually, or on a blackboard or overhead projector transparency if you are in a group. Then agree through discussion on a series of graphic symbols to put into these bars to create a score. Exact pitches may be less accurate than those of the printed score (though, if someone can identify them with the help, perhaps, of perfect pitch, by all means write them in.) But the structural relationships which give coherence and impetus to the opening of the Quintet may be 'notated' in a far more sophisticated way than is available in a conventionally notated score.

Now—and only now!—you may *look* at Ex. 8.2a, and assess how far your 'score' is superior to it.

8.3 Long-term structures

Short-lived structural relationships such as the sense of acceleration created by a bar of crotchets followed by a bar of quavers, or even the repetition of a nine-bar sentence, are easily recognized once we are alerted to them. Longer structures are more difficult to grasp. Certainly, in longer-term listening you should not expect anything like the detail extracted from the first seventeen bars of the Mozart Clarinet Quintet, though absorbing much of that detail becomes less laboured as you get more accustomed to doing it.

Exercise and discussion

This exercise should be done on a much more expansive basis than the last. It is concerned with establishing broad areas of musical activity.

Draw seventy-nine bars on a blank piece of paper—lines of four bars will give enough space to work in. Then play a recording of the exposition of the Mozart Clarinet Quintet with one person calling out bar numbers up to bar 79. While this is happening, perhaps for a second or third time, put down a few markers either graphically or with words. So, bar 19 = solo clarinet; bar 26 = similar, but 'cello; bar 35 = dialogue of that solo begins, and so on.

Aim first for the main events like striking changes of texture, rhythm, timbre, dynamics.

Do the exercise now, before reading on.

Next, discuss your 'score' with one or two others, adding anything they have noticed which escaped your attention; these exercises are *not* competitive.

Ex. 8.2a Quintet for Clarinet and Strings in A (K581), W. A. Mozart (1756–91)

Finally, read on. Your score may have identified some of the major events such as:

b 19—introduction to extended clarinet melody;
b 26—introduction to similar 'cello melody;
b 35—introduction of clarinet/violin dialogue;
b 42—new accompanying texture ('cello pizz.);
b 49—new accompanying texture (off-beat) and change to minor mode;
b 57—new accompanying figure (off-beat quavers);
b 64—trill leading to new dynamic + melody;
b 75—reference to opening minims.

Next, having identified some of the broad contours of the exposition, listen to the whole movement. This time, do not use barlines but instead draw broad areas on a blank piece of paper to create an unfocused 'score'. Listen two or three times; compare notes with others; then (and only then) read on:

1. After the exposition, with which you will now be fairly familiar, a brief modulating reflection leads to the opening music again, in a foreign key.
2. The violin takes the clarinet's arpeggio and arabesques and begins a series of entries until all the strings are playing.
3. As the clarinet begins an accompanying wide arpeggio, the semiquaver 'arabesque' figure becomes continuous from top to bottom of the strings in turn.
4. A new series of entries climbs up through the quintet culminating in a quiet sustained moment above off-beat quavers in the middle strings, returning in mood and key to the recapitulation.
5. The recapitulation repeats the musical material of the exposition but with some striking differences. Comparison with your 'score' of the exposition should show where and what they are.

If this were an exercise in analysis from a score, it would be considered absurdly superficial, and there is no suggestion that much deeper analysis, with the score as a visual aid, is not desirable. But this exercise in *listening* rather than seeing and reading provides a sense of the span and the perspective of the movement which visual analysis can obscure. It forces ears to hear rather than eyes to see, and it focuses attention on the interaction of all the musical elements rather than only on the visually exact symbols of pitches, rhythms and a few approximate dynamics and phrasings.

Feel free, though, to examine the score of the Mozart Clarinet Quintet as soon as you have decided to end this experiment in analysis which depends wholly on the ear. Until then, the exercise can be taken as much further as you like. The process of identifying the kind of detail extracted from the first seventeen bars (section 8.2) could be extended to the whole movement. But experience warns that the exercise can be made so intense that it becomes counter-productive—so it is perhaps time to extend the repertoire, in this process of larger-scale structural analysis.

8.4 Structure and time-scale

Much music in the western classical tradition is written within forms which are conventional, and so predictable. 'Sonata form' is the most common. More recent music is frequently cast in forms which composers devise uniquely for each single piece so we cannot listen, at a first hearing, with any expectation of a predictable series of sections, creating a conventional overall form within which to perceive the composer's structural relationships. Without the security of knowing in advance that we are, for example, experiencing new musical ideas in an exposition, exploring the potential within the ideas in a development, or meeting them with deeper understanding in a recapitulation, it becomes all the more essential to recognize the way in which musical ideas unfold and grow. Otherwise they can simply drift past us as a series of mildly pleasant sensations.

One vital aid to discerning new overall structures is to know how long they last. As we listen to a middle-period Haydn symphony, new to us, we none the less know that the first movement will last about six to eight minutes. If it is markedly shorter or longer we probably notice it and it becomes a matter for comment, and even for assessing when the symphony might have

101

been written. With a new piece by a present-day composer we have no such security: all programme notes should include mention of the duration of each movement or section so that we know within what scale to set our bearings and to expect structural unities to appear. CD discs are helpful in this respect as they usually state the length of each track in the accompanying notes.

Exercise and discussion

The aim now is to discern a broad structure in a piece which does not use a classical convention such as binary, sonata or rondo form. You will need a recording of the *Musique Funèbre* (1958) of Witold Lutoslawski [EMI CDM5 65076-2]—on the assumption that you are not already familiar with it. The exercise can, of course, be done with any unfamiliar piece of music, but it is helpful at least to begin with the *Musique Funèbre* and the description of what you may find in it, simply as an example of how to tackle the process of broad-scale structural listening.

Play once through the middle section, entitled 'Métamorphoses'. It begins about 3 minutes and 55 seconds into the piece, with the first pizzicato in the work. The previous texture has collapsed to a *pp* 'perdendosi' bass F and a bar of silence. The section lasts about 4 minutes and 40 seconds. Take a broad view and aim, first, to do no more than identify a number of sections of different kinds of musical activity. The title of the movement, 'Métamorphoses', will warn you that changes from one section to the next are not immediate—the edges are blurred.

Listen now: do not read on until you have heard the 4 minutes 40 seconds section, say, three times. Have pencil and paper ready to jot down aids to memory as you listen. Between each hearing, discuss freely if you are working in a group, so that you alert one another to ideas which may need confirmation or rejection at the next hearing. You may have concluded that the music falls into nine sections though each one is 'metamorphosed' into the next and the divisions are so diffused that some are barely perceptible.

1. Pizzicatos climb from double-basses up to violins, overlapping with—

2. a bowed singing figure. At its climax—
3. quavers begin, at the top of the range, disturbed first by unpredictable accented chords, then by—
4. regular accents in the middle of the texture.
5. Semiquaver groups appear, mainly falling and, again, at the top of the range, each group expanding on the previous one until they fuse together continuously. Then, below them, appear—
6. tremolo interjections with contrasting sustained notes beginning with strong crescendos and diminuendos. As these fade away,
7. rising tremolo scales gradually invade the texture, expanding to tremolo arpeggios around—
8. a four-note semiquaver group, falling and rising again. Then over increasingly dense and loud tremolos, to—
9. final accents and a huge tremolo crescendo to the densest chord available in the western chromatic system: it uses all twelve notes simultaneously, over a range of more than five octaves.

8.5 Structure through timbre

Lutoslawski creates the contrasts between the sections of the 'Métamorphoses' by using the musical elements in a quite 'classically' conventional way. Rhythms accelerate, melodic motifs appear in imitation creating textures and densities which pass quite predictably across the range of the string orchestra.

For an exercise which focuses on the elements in quite different proportions, you could listen to all, or part (the first 3 minutes 30 seconds) of *Lontano* by György Ligeti [WERG WER60163-50].

Here, *timbre* is by far the most telling element. There are few identifiable rhythmic cells, very little in the way of melodic motifs let alone extended melody. Although pitches are very precisely notated, unlike those of the Penderecki *Threnody* (examined in section 3.7) they create a subtle range of densities, textures and timbres. This, too, is an excellent piece of which to make a structural analysis. It will be very different from that of

103

the Mozart Clarinet Quintet, probably much less detailed and reflecting Ligeti's intention to focus on 'web-like sound-complexes' (his words) rather than on audibly perceivable intervals and rhythms. He uses the analogy of a chemical compound, where all the elements are *fused* in contrast to a *mixture* of elements without any chemical reaction to conceal their separate identities—read the programme note on the record sleeve.

8.6 Structure in performance

So far these exercises in discerning the simultaneous structural relationships of elements and the structures which shape musical events through time, 'vertical' and 'horizontal' structure, have all been from the point of view of the listener. Equally important is to apply the principles to your own playing, and to your own composition. The processes will be essentially the same except that now you have some control over the musical outcome.

Exercise and discussion

Refer again to section 8.2 for guidance about how you might identify and assess structural detail through considering each *element* in turn, how they are manipulated (repetition, alteration, etc.) and how they interact—for example, the tension of an accent being created by combining an articulatory silence, a sforzando and changes in density and range.

After refreshing your memory in this way, have someone play the opening half-minute or so, perhaps sixteen bars, of whatever he or she is currently learning—a Grade 1 piano piece or a folk melody on descant recorder are just as suitable as a concerto solo.

Discuss and note down, graphically or using some conventional notation, what you hear. How far did it reflect its structural potential? Were musical *repetitions*, exact, or varied like sequences, performed with precisely repeated bowing/articulation and phrasing/dynamic shape/timbre? How far were contrasting *alterations* made clear—were staccatos vigorous enough, legatos wholly even? Should they have been? If so, why? If not, why not?

Then discuss your conclusions with the performer, in a constructive and sympathetic way! The aim is to expand the imagination and strengthen confidence rather than to undermine it with mocking criticism or derision.

This exercise can be done as often as you wish, perhaps giving a turn to every performer in the group. Extend the length of the extracts, to a minute, to a complete exposition, to a whole movement, to expand your sense of structure—focused long-term listening and performing is one of the most difficult levels of musical awareness to achieve. It is easy enough to imitate the phrasing of two adjacent phrases, but much harder to relate a sonata 'first-subject' melody to every mutation of it in a development, and then reproduce it exactly as before in the recapitulation.

The whole exercise can also be done by one person alone, though it is clearly harder to stimulate as many ideas as may arise when several people are contributing to a lively discussion. Ultimately, though, we are dependent on ourselves alone, as performers and, particularly, as composers, in all the creative judgements we make. So structural analyses can be done as described in the exercises below.

8.7 Do-it-yourself exercises

First, make a written analysis (using whatever graphic or notational conventions best suit your needs) of a recording of a short section from a piece of music in a style with which you are familiar enough for it to be accessible. Then write another analysis of the same music, but now complete. Avoid the detail you will have found in the first extract. Instead, take a broad view and limit yourself first to the half-dozen or so markers which delineate the overall structure. These might include a double-bar and repeat, the entries of a concerto soloist, the verses/choruses of a folk song, the solo 'breaks' in a jazz ensemble, significant changes in speed or metre. Only after several hearings, and once the main 'landmarks' are fixed, should you change, as it were, to a higher magnification, and fill in more detail. It is the broad view, needing extended musical memory and an awareness of lengthy spans of time, which is difficult to grasp.

Second, take a piece of music which you have already learned to play to a high standard and so know well. Using the score as little as possible, and only to remind yourself of the order of the main musical events, *think* through the piece, identifying any structural relationships you can find. Note them down on a piece of paper and ask yourself how far you are conscious of them as you play. For example, if a phrase from the opening returns later, do you phrase it in the same way, with the same fingering/bowing/tonguing/dynamic shape and accents/tone colour? Should you—or is there a structural reason for altering your interpretation of it?

Third, listen to two (or more) different recordings of a piece. There are plenty to choose from: 35 sets of *Brandenburg Concertos* in the record catalogues as I write, and over one hundred recordings of the 'Hallelujah' chorus since recording was invented! Does one performance display structural relationships better than the other? Listen to phrasing and articulation, balance between parts such as melody and accompaniment or several 'voices' in counterpoint, metrical pace, the relative loudness and softness of dynamics, the timbral qualities of instruments or voices.

Finally, listen to a strophic pop song. Seek differences between the successive verses and choruses. If they exist, note them down.

9

Imaging

9.1 Reading by ear and by eye

There are two ways of 'reading' music. One is to see its symbols and react mentally and physically to them straight on to an instrument. The other is to convert the symbols into *imagined* sound, inside your head. The first of these ways is perfectly valid and in fact, for almost everyone, is the more reliable means of discovering the pitches involved in melody and harmony. There are very few musicians who can pick up a score and imagine it accurately. Those with 'perfect pitch' may get close to 'hearing' this pitch element but for many there is little more than a general sense of metrical and rhythmic flow at a first silent 'reading'. So by all means play music through as one way to begin to learn it.

However, the second approach, silent 'reading', can uncover things which performance-reading may overlook. When we are taught to sight-read on an instrument, we are usually encouraged to 'get the notes right' as the first priority. It is very common, for instance, to hear wrong notes re-played to correct them, creating a kind of musical stammer. This, of course, totally destroys the accuracy of all the musical elements except pitch. Correcting a 'wrong note' disturbs metre and rhythm, the legato of a phrase, the dynamic level (corrections are usually accented!), and so, in turn, texture, timbre, the pace of events, all are distorted. Silent reading, or 'imaging', on the other hand, allows us to focus on non-pitch elements while concerning ourselves less with accurate pitching of notes in linear melody and vertical harmony.

This is not to say that we should abandon all attempts to read pitches silently to ourselves, in our heads. It is a very valuable skill, and one probably best developed by singing. Take every opportunity for this, particularly if you can find a choir with a conductor who insists on unaccompanied sight-singing as a means of learning the notes. This forces singers to 'image', or form notes in the mind, rather than respond to piano notes a split second after hearing them. At least, this will develop your ability to pitch the successive notes of a single melodic line accurately and rhythmically.

So this chapter is not about an *alternative* to accuracy in imaging pitch. Rather, it is intended to complement that skill and redress the balance, adding to silent reading of pitches all the other musical elements and the structural relationships between them, which together combine to approach a total musical experience. It is as important to read the unison texture, the *ff* dynamic, the low string timbre and density and the rhythm of the opening of Beethoven's Fifth Symphony as it is to read there the pitches of a major third; Beethoven himself expands it to a perfect fifth at the start of the second subject.

Another very practical reason for deepening our imaging ability is that we need access to all music, not merely to that which we can play, sing, or reach through hearing recordings. No one could be a student of literature without being able to read and interpret language from its written symbols. A rough analogy can be made with the study of music: we need some ability to read and interpret its written symbols. We would be severely handicapped if we were solely dependent on live or recorded performance to give us access to the subject.

9.2 Exercise and discussion

Working in pairs, give yourselves the pitch of any note—this is not a pitching exercise. Then, one person 'composes' that note for the other to play or sing. It might be a semibreve for a violinist, marked 'arco sfz ＞ p, con molto vibrato'. For a singer, it could be marked 'mp, ⌢, ➤ niente, to the shifting vowels "oo-ah-ee" '.

The composer images the note—develops a clear mental impression of what is expected. The performer thinks carefully about all the implications of the notation, and then plays/sings it. If the composer's expectations are exactly fulfilled, the communication with the performer has been successful. If not, as is very likely, something is wrong.

Discuss where any misunderstandings have arisen. Did the composer write imprecisely? Was the performer's interpretation wrong? Is conventional notation simply unequal to the task of communicating every nuance of even a single note?

With or without the guidance of a teacher, this exercise can be made simpler or more sophisticated, to suit the level of a student's imaging skills. It is as relevant to the National Curriculum requirement that 'pupils should be given opportunities to communicate musical ideas to others' as to an intending professional musician at conservatoire or university.

As an example of a more searching kind of imaging, find an F natural. By now, perhaps, constant practising of the strategies suggested in section 5.3 has developed in you an acceptable approximation to perfect pitch. Otherwise, use piano, tuning fork or another reliable source of pitch. Read through Ex. 9.2a—do *not* read further until you have done so.

Next, discuss in pairs or threes what you heard . . . and again, do not read on!

After the discussion, some of the questions which may have arisen in it are

1. Did you hear a horn?
2. If so, who was playing it? Did you mentally hear the velvet smoothness and almost legendary accuracy of Dennis Brain for whom the part was written in 1943? Or was it a rough-toned amateur performance?
3. How close or distant was the imagined performer?
4. Did you find a close approximation to 'Andante (crotchet = 80)', and, within that, how far was the metre of your imagined performance *sempre ad libitum*?

Ex. 9.2a 'Prologue' from *Serenade for Tenor, Horn and Strings*, Op. 31, Benjamin Britten (1913–76)

Horn in F

5. Where exactly did the metrical pulse bend and flex?
6. How loud was the first note?
7. How firmly was it tongued?
8. Was the sustained third note coloured with a vibrato?
9. If so, how wide and fast was it?
10. How long was the first comma at the end of bar 1?
11. How smooth were the slurred intervals from bar 2 onwards?
. . . and so on—the range of questions is almost endless.

In fact, it is common to discover that most people engaging in such an exercise hear a kind of vocalized sound or a barely audible whistle made by pitching within their mouths but without using vocal chords. Identifying pitches can often totally obscure every other notated element, let alone the un-notated qualities implied by 'Horn in F (Dennis Brain 1943) . . .'.

Unless you are a horn player, you will probably be surprised by a phenomenon which Britten capitalized upon here. He specified, in a footnote, 'The Prologue to be played on natural harmonics', without using valves, so the pitches of some notes, F and A in particular, are out of tune—so wildly that you may well feel they affect the timbre of what you hear: the musical elements interact with each other. As another example, the relationship between dynamics and timbre were noted in Chapter 2.7.

Repeat the exercise, now that you are alerted to the musical potential of these fourteen bars.

9.3 Do-it-yourself exercise

Concentrate for a week on identifying the range of tone colours, at various points in its compass and played by different performers, of the french horn, using recordings, listening to live performances in orchestral or band rehearsals, discussing with any horn-playing friends. And this, of course, is only an example. A week spent concentrating on violins and violinists, oboes and oboists, pop vocalists, or jazz pianists will extend your repertoire of sound and enhance your ability to 'image' it. Then, in turn, it is available for you to use, as a composer in your instructions to players, as a performer in the imagination you can bring to bear upon the written notes you play, or as a listener enjoying or suffering performances of the compositions of others.

9.4 Imaging interpretation

The imaging exercise in section 9.2 can be taken further if you have *two* recordings of the Britten *Serenade* (see 6.3), or of anything else of manageable scale for that matter. The texture of a complete symphony orchestra will probably be too complex a challenge to respond to with much success, but a few bars of any solo instrument, or of the solo part of an accompanied sonata, is perfectly suitable.

111

Imaging

Create a mental image of your ideal performance and then compare it with the recordings. Jot down any conclusions and share them in discussion with others.

9.5 Imaging beyond the written notes

It may have occurred to you that so far, in this chapter, you have not been invited to *perform*. Yet all the activities and exercises have been contributing to a deeper level of musical perception, not of exact pitch but in terms of all the other elements which too often are obscured by our concern to 'get the notes right'. In fact, this is an object lesson for performers. A great deal can be learnt about a piece of music by *not* performing it but, instead, sitting away from your instrument and reading through it in your head. Accuracy of notes recedes into the background—if you already know the piece, they are, anyway, easily 'thought' correctly—and instead you can pay attention to the other elements, in great detail and with great clarity.

Do-it-yourself exercise

Take a piece of music which you are about to learn but which as yet is wholly unfamiliar to you. Read through it, silently, away from your instrument. Take particular note of all the elements which are easy to read: precise pitches may be obscure; harmonic progressions may not form themselves inside your head; but '*ff*', a slur, a staccato dot, the rise and fall of a melodic phrase, the density of a low-pitched many-note chord or the transparency of a widely spaced two-part texture—all these are immediately obvious to the eye. So prepare your interpretation of the music before you actually hear it at all, even for the first time. Be daring. Think a forte really loud, a piano really soft; think a big articulatory silence between two phrases; think a penetrating cantabile timbre in a melody, set against a much less colourful accompaniment. By doing this exercise regularly, before any new piece is learnt, it may be that your interpretations will become more bold, your playing less cautious and pallid. It is a very well-known phenomenon that a performer believes a confident

112

crescendo perhaps, or an accent, has been made, but an audience is quite unaware of the intention, let alone the effect. Test this by recording your own performance, to discover whether, when you become your own audience, elements which you thought you were expressing prominently appear to fade into insignificance. If so, reading such elements silently will help your mind to focus on them, and your performances to endow them with the same level of importance that we conventionally attach to playing right notes.

This exercise is just as important for composers. They too are often concerned most of all to get the right pitches down on paper, forgetting the importance of all the other symbols which create musical effects. Concentrating on these to the temporary exclusion of pitches will help to ensure that they take their proper place in the final fair copy of the score of an original composition.

9.6 Exercises and discussion

Our ability to 'image' in our heads what we see on the page can be developed by breaking down the whole process into separate constituent parts. The following exercises and discussion require of you great concentration—and great honesty! No one but you can know how far you are achieving their aims.

Ex. 9.6a

First, read the note in Ex. 9.6a. As you do so, 'image' it as

1. an A played at half-a-dozen different dynamic levels on a piano;
2. the same note at the same dynamic levels on a violin/trumpet/flute/harpsichord;
3. the same note, at various dynamic levels, on various instruments, but repeated in a regular beat ($\frac{2}{4}$, $\frac{3}{4}$, $\frac{6}{8}$), at various

113

speeds (MM = 60, MM = 90, MM = 120), with accents on first/second notes, from staccatissimo to legato.

This exercise, valuable as it is to performers, is particularly important to you as a composer, emphasizing the range of possible implications within a single musical symbol, a crotchet A.

Second, pitching accuracy can be developed silently, too. Have someone write, on a stave-lined board or an overhead projector, the A of Ex. 9.6a. Identify its actual pitch from a tuning fork or any other reliable source. Then, as someone, tutor or student, writes additional notes, image them—hear them absolutely silently—until, after four or five of them, you sing loudly and confidently the note you believe you have arrived at. Pace the difficulty of intervals and the number of them, as in Ex. 9.6b, to begin with, and then Ex. 9.6c (*considerably* later).

Ex. 9.6b

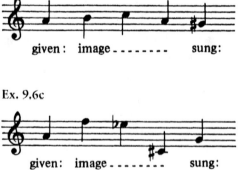

Ex. 9.6c

This whole exercise can be turned into a party game, provided that competitiveness does not induce demoralization and loss of confidence among those who do not win it. It can also be done by individuals on their own: sound a note and sing it; think an interval from it and sing that; continue this for a while and then check on a piano to see if you have arrived accurately at where you expected to be.

Third, 'image' the chord of Ex. 9.6d, having been given an E♭ from a stable source of pitch.

Ex. 9.6d

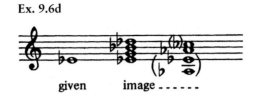

Resolve it in your head to A♭ major, then to A♭ minor. 'Image' the same notes spelled differently: Ex. 9.6e.

Ex. 9.6e

Resolve it to a ⁶₄ chord on D, i.e. treat it as a German sixth chord in G major/minor. Extend the exercise to imaging several consecutive chords creating harmonic progressions. As far as possible, think horizontally, following the linear flow of the parts. In common-practice tonal harmony, for instance, leading notes can be expected to rise, sevenths to fall. So the imaging of Ex. 9.6f is helped by a consciousness of such conventions: Ex. 9.6f.

Ex. 9.6f

1. sevenths normally fall;
2. leading notes normally rise;

3. the supertonic chord generally progresses to the dominant, so the bass here is most likely to move up by step;
4. the most likely resolution of a dominant seventh is to the tonic, and the stronger bass leap is downwards;
5. dominant sevenths fall, often to . . .
6. the *tierce de Picardie*, a common cliché at a final cadence.

In so far as notes cannot be absorbed absolutely simultaneously, read from the bottom upwards: the bass supports, and so in a sense determines, the probable harmony above it.

Finally, after considerable slow practice on progressions short and predictable enough to be manageable, this exercise can extend to the imaging of whole pieces such as four-part homophonic hymns or, more contrapuntally complex, Bach chorale harmonizations.

9.7 Access to music through imaging

So far the imaging exercises have largely been intended to uncover and clarify elements in music we may well intend to perform. The other practical reason for developing imaging skill is to make accessible to us music which we cannot play, alone at least. This is a particular reason for reading scores of music for larger forces, though conductors will read these, as instrumentalists read their single parts, as preparation for performing them.

9.8 Exercises and discussion

First, image Ex. 9.8a. This is intentionally selected to be daunting as far as pitches are concerned. Few musicians could read them accurately. It therefore focuses attention on all the other elements. Spend five minutes extracting as much information about the sound of these first ten bars as possible. Work in pairs or groups of three and discuss freely what you are discerning from the written symbols. Begin now—though, if the exercise is too intimidating, read through the following hints to assist you.

Ex. 9.8a Symphony, Op. 21, Anton Webern (1883–1945)

*) Sounding as written

Ex. 9.8a *cont.*

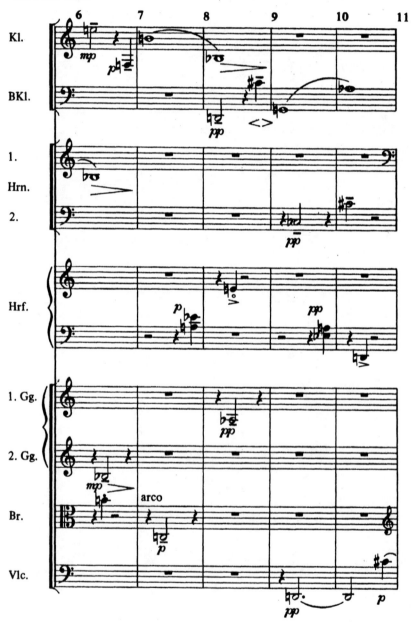

1. 'Ruhig schreitend' means 'moving quietly'.
2. 'Minim = ca 50' can be calculated with the help of the tricks suggested in section 4.7.
3. The nine instruments (clarinet, bass clarinet, two horns, harp and string quartet) are all notated at sounding pitch—there are no transposed parts to deal with.
4. Think through, one by one, the timbral qualities you would expect from these instruments. Take into account where in their compass they are playing—this greatly influences tone colour (section 2.5).
5. Note the dynamic markings, ranging only from *pp* to *mp*.
6. Note the playing techniques required—pizzicato and arco, with and without tenuto marks.
7. Think through the rhythms created by these largely detached notes, but observe the three legato leaps of an augmented octave/minor ninth.
8. You will be helped by discovering structural patterns: the horns are playing a mirror canon, as also are the clarinets. . . .

When you believe you have imaged the sound of these ten bars with some degree of accuracy, hear a recording of them [DG 423 254-2].

This exercise can be applied to any available music, of course. Only ensure that the early attempts at imaging a full score are of something sufficiently atonal to steer you away from concentrating too much on exact pitches—on 'getting the notes right'. There are so many more kinds of information to be distilled out of a score once your attention is drawn to them.

However, once the point is made that imaging is about more than pitches, and when you have worked through the challenge of the Webern Symphony, Op. 21—and anything else you chose to add to it—by all means turn to imaging precise pitches as an integral part of further reading. An example is the opening of Beethoven's Symphony No. 2 in D, Op. 36 (Ex. 9.8b). Again, take advantage of every clue offered by the printed page.

1. Adagio molto at an editorially suggested 'quaver = 84'.
2. The instruments called for and the timbre of each of them individually, and of all of them together, at the ranges

119

Ex. **9.8b** Symphony No. 2 in D, Op. 36, L. van Beethoven (1770–1827)

at which they are playing. (The timbral quality will be influenced by the date, 1803, of the first performance: if possible, include an 'authentic' performance among the recordings you use to check your imaging of timbre.)

3. The dynamics, fiercely contrasting and influencing the timbres.
4. Such structural devices as the slurs and the broader phrasing.
5. The rhythms within the $\frac{3}{4}$ metre.
6. On this occasion, the pitches creating melody (first oboe to begin with), homophonic accompaniment (second oboe and bassoons for four bars) and interacting motifs (especially from bar 9).

This example was selected partly because, though less familiar than some other symphonic openings of similar stature and manageable speed, there are plenty of recordings available. If you have access to more than one [DG 439 001-2 and ARCH 439 900-2] it would be interesting to discover if any of the audible differences between them were predicted by you as you pieced together your image of the sounds symbolized by the printed notes.

9.9 Do-it-yourself exercises

As the whole imaging process is such a personal one, it all lends itself very well to doing alone without the benefit of discussion. So take any printed music which you do not already know but of which you have access to a recording or which you can play on your own instrument when the exercise is complete.

Selecting only as much as is manageable, begin piecing together a mental image of it. If a full score is too complicated, consider only a string section, a pair of clarinets, or a single line. If eight bars is too long for your memory to retain the image, take only four bars, or two. As throughout this book, you should devise exercises which, while they challenge you, are always within the limits of what you can successfully achieve. You gain nothing from failure; each achievement on the other hand can serve as a basis for the next.

10

Playing by ear

10.1 Externalizing

Chapter 9, 'Imaging', was concerned with internal processes, with generating an impression of sound in the mind. In this chapter the aim is to add to that internal process a further stage, of *externalizing* sound accurately through instruments. Externalizing is something we constantly do with the voice. Children learn nursery rhymes by first listening, and then singing what they have heard. To some extent we do the same when learning to play an instrument. Most teachers demonstrate what is required, both physically and musically, in any particular musical situation; conductors verbalize articulation and sing phrasings in order to communicate their intentions.

Yet strangely little instrumental playing by ear is demanded in conventional aural training. In general, the music which is fed in to our ears is then responded to on paper (so-called 'dictation'), or vocally (with such requirements as singing the lower of two parts played on the piano, for example), or in words (the interval *heard* is *called* a 'perfect fifth', the piece *heard* was *written* in the 'Classical period' or in 'binary form' . . .).

All of these responses to what we hear can be some use to us. The exercises in this chapter are additional, not alternative, to them; they are designed to focus attention on playing what we *hear*, rather than only what we *see* in a score or are *told* by a teacher or conductor. Thus they may appear to be exclusively relevant to performers. In fact, composers need an understanding of them too in order, for instance, to refine their understanding of how instruments may relate to one another. Many details of compositional structure (Chapter 8) depend on how faithfully instruments can imitate, alter or develop each others' musical materials.

10.2 Exercises and discussion

First, one person invents a rhythmic pattern lasting, say, two bars: keep it simple. Then the composer plays it on his or her instrument, to be imitated immediately, within a constant pulse, by the next performer (who may well be using a different instrument). The two-bar pattern is thus passed right round the group. Note two important points:

1. The requirement is not simply to imitate a pattern of crotchets and quavers but to reproduce faithfully every nuance of what has just been heard. If the first player inadvertently accents the second crotchet, the second player must accent it too, to precisely the same degree. If the second player minutely delays a quaver by accident, that is then the model to be imitated by the third player, and so on.
2. As this pattern is passed round and round the group, like a message in 'Chinese whispers', each player must remember exactly how he or she played it last time and notice, and be ready to demonstrate, how it has varied by the time it gets round again. Resist the temptation to return to the initial pattern, to 'put right' other players' 'mistakes'. The aim is to allow the pattern to go through a process of evolution, changing constantly through the chance 'mutations' which human error will subject it to.

The exercise can be done by as few as two people, passing the pattern to and fro. However, the fewer performers involved, the more frequently it will return to each one and so the harder it becomes to allow the pattern to evolve rather than to regress to how it began.

Second, repeat this exercise, but this time using a melodic pattern, perhaps initially in equal crotchets for simplicity. Announce the first note and use a compass which, with octave transpositions to allow tuba and piccolo players and the like to take part, will suit everyone. Again, do not correct errors—'mutations'—so that the melody may well evolve. The imitations should be as faithful as before, taking in minute changes of rhythm as well as accidents which alter pitches.

Third, it is not unlikely that, despite the emphasis throughout this book on expressive elements other than the pitch and duration of notes, the musical fragments composed and passed around in the two previous exercises will have lacked articulations, slurs and phrasing, dynamics, or such calculated timbral qualities as a particular speed of vibrato or placing of a bow. So add these to the rhythmic and pitch patterns of the first two exercises, while also increasing the length of the music to four bars or even more, as your skill at imitating each other by ear becomes greater and your aural awareness deepens.

Fourth, a rather more subtle exercise is valuable not only for giving practice in playing by ear but also in analysing your own interpretation of a piece of music. Play an extract from a piece on which you are currently working. Make the extract short enough—even a single bar—for another instrumentalist to be able to play it back by ear. Although this exercise approaches the situation of a teacher demonstrating to a pupil, and so is best done by two people who play the same instrument, it may also be revealing to use dissimilar instruments—a flute imitating a violin, a trumpet imitating a 'cello. The point of the exercise is not only to test the *second* player's ability to imitate the first, but also for the *first* player and any other listeners to assess how accurate such an imitation has been. Pitches and rhythms may have been correct—but what of phrasing, of accents and dynamics . . . ? Often the first player may believe that the music has been inaccurately *imitated* while, in fact, he or she did not actually *perform* it as intended. In effect, this is similar to making a recording of yourself and analysing what you hear on playing it back. Now, though, your 'interpretation' will be further 'interpreted' by another performer and perhaps your exaggerations will be caricatured or your honest attempts to be deeply expressive will prove to be half-hearted or inaudible.

The fifth exercise helps to develop the ability to do two things at once. This is constantly needed by performing musicians, for example when playing your own part but concentrating on a conductor, or listening, for ensemble, balance, intonation and more, to what is being played around you. Each person in the group composes a rhythm in an agreed metre and through an agreed number of bars (say two to begin with, though the exercise can be expanded almost indefinitely). Write this rhythm down. Then have two performers play their rhythms simultaneously to each other, on a monotone, while concentrating on learning the *other* person's rhythm. Immediately continue, without interrupting the constant metre, by playing the other person's rhythm by ear. Ex. 10.2a will demonstrate.

Ex. 10.2a

Compose in written notation, then play by reading while learning other player's rhythm ‖ play, by imitation

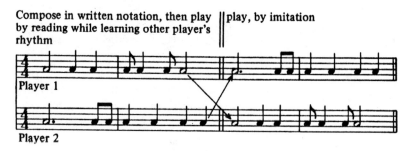

Player 1

Player 2

The sixth exercise is, predictably perhaps, to do the same with two fragments of melody.

Although these exercises can be expanded to tax an experienced professional musician (and may already do so!), they are all open to simplifying for use long before sixth form, university or conservatoire. Primary school pupils play imitatively—even clapping patterns in echo is 'playing by ear'.

10.3 Adapting exercises to ensure success

Both these last two exercises in section 10.2 are difficult, initially at least. If they prove daunting, shorten and simplify them. Ex.

10.3a may be quite enough to begin with. Yet a member of a first-rate string quartet can be playing a line from Beethoven's *Grosse Fuge*, Op. 133, while sufficiently aware of three colleagues' lines to achieve a flexible but exact ensemble of timing, intonation, dynamics, tone and balance—all the elements, in fact, which combine in a great performance of such an extremely taxing work.

Ex. 10.3a

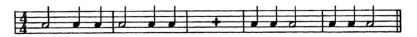

10.4 Instrumental applications

Read again section 5.4 and the first exercise in section 5.5, but now play rather than sing chords, alter them and, finally, alternate between your own chosen note in a chord and your neighbour's. You will probably need to be led by a conductor, to stop and start the chords.

10.5 Further instrumental exercises

Using the procedures described in sections 5.6 and 5.7, work through those exercises but, again, using instruments rather than voices. The final exercise described in section 5.7 is particularly challenging. It is, for many people, a great deal harder to reproduce a melody by ear through an instrument than with the voice. If necessary, go back to section 10.2 and practise the second exercise (playing back a heard melody by ear) and the sixth exercise (learning one melody while playing another).

10.6 Playing as a stage in transcription

Playing by ear is an invaluable skill for arrangers and composers. Music students have traditionally been expected to sit in silence, writing music in their own style or imitating that of someone else in pastiche composition or arrangement. While this certainly helps to develop skill at imaging and writing down the musical symbols for what is being heard silently in the head, it is not actually the process used by most composers who unashamedly have a sound source available to them to test and manipulate sounds as they work. At one extreme of compositional method, in the electro-acoustic studio, the process of composing often links together very closely indeed the generating of audible sounds and manipulating them, a voice at a time, into a complete digital recording.

Exercise

This exercise is relevant to anyone dealing with existing music, as an arranger or transcriber. Take as short a fragment of recorded music, written for your own instrument, as you can manage. As little as two bars of a Haydn piano minuet or a dance movement from the Bach 'Cello Suites, of a rock bass guitar solo or a traditional jazz chorus—all these or anything similar will serve the purpose initially, until your perception develops further with practice.

1. Play the recording a few times. (CD recordings are the best source as you can cue the machine very accurately. Trying to hit on the right groove of an LP record or find the place with the less exact counter of a cassette player can be so distracting that the object of the exercise is lost. Alternatively, use the beginning of a record—easily cued—or record your chosen fragment onto the beginning of a cassette tape.)
2. Play what you have heard, on your own instrument. Feel free to 'doodle', to fumble for the right notes, if they do not occur to you immediately.
3. Write down what you have just played. This will be easier than conventional dictation as you will have identified exact pitches on your instrument rather than having to distinguish them in your head.
4. Check what you have written by playing the recording again, and by comparing your manuscript with the printed score if one is available. Confirmation of rock, jazz and other music not normally notated will have to be by ear alone.

10.7 Do-it-yourself exercises

First, imagine a rhythm in your head. Begin with something simple like four crotchets in $\frac{4}{4}$ time, continued for several bars. Then play it, but not unthinkingly—ensure that you are playing what you are thinking, 'playing by (inner) ear', rather than mindlessly repeating a crotchet beat on 'autopilot', as it were. Increase the complexity of the rhythms as far as you can, so long as you are always playing what you have positively planned to play.

Second, imagine some intervals or an extended melody in your head, either without or with some of the rhythmic sophistication you may be building up in the previous exercise. Then play it. If you can do so successfully, compose in your head a longer or more angular melody and then play it. Again, aim to get it as correct as possible first time through; avoid too much fumbling for notes. But always set the task towards the limits of what you can achieve so that you are challenging yourself to improve.

Third, hear a recording of a short section, four, eight or sixteen bars, of a piece you are learning and which, through this section at least, you can play from memory. Assuming pitches and rhythms are securely memorized, focus your attention on the other elements and then reproduce them, still playing by ear. Imitate dynamic variations, articulations and tone qualities as exactly as possible.

Finally, in the light of experiencing the third exercise, compose more melodies but ensure now that they have a planned range of dynamics, of accents and phrasings, of instrumental timbres. Ensure that you perform them faithfully when you play your mental composition.

11

Improvisation

11.1 The need for improvisation

Chapter 10 was concerned with imitating instrumental performances. Most of the do-it-yourself exercises, though, involved
imitating music which existed only in your mind. As soon as this
process is virtually instantaneous, it becomes improvisation.

This exists at various levels of freedom. For example, the
extempore realization at the keyboard of a baroque figured bass
is very strictly controlled indeed. No notes foreign to the
intended chord are permitted except as decoration; every disso-
nance indicated must be properly prepared, sounded and
resolved; clear conventions exist about acceptable range and
compass, and the balance of volume and timbre to be achieved
with the obbligato instruments. A solo 'break' in traditional jazz,
however, allows freedom in every respect except adherence to a
planned harmonic scheme, though the exercise of that freedom
is a matter of taste and judgement which determines the esteem
in which a performer is held.

A classical concerto cadenza is less controlled again. All that is
specified is the final resolution, through a trill, of the $^6_4$ chord which
signalled the start of the extemporization. The only constraints
between these two points are conventions—of length, of musical
material being related to the body of the movement, and so on.

At the other extreme is almost total freedom. Those French
and Dutch organists who end their recitals with an extempor-

ization are limited only by the nature of the original theme which they invent to improvise upon. Some composers of today's *avant garde* invite us to perform quite spontaneously within the most generalized constraints; John Cage's *Variations IV* (1963) is for 'any number of players, any sounds or combinations of sounds produced by any means . . .'—all the choices are left to the performers who are wholly at liberty to play unprepared, to improvise.

In one sense, *all* performance involves improvisation except for music composed straight on to tape or computer disc, where the only improvisatory freedom is experienced once, by the composer as he or she composes. In every other case there is some degree of freedom to vary the music from one performance to the next. Indeed, it is this improvisatory, unpredictable quality which makes live performance so exciting to performers and listeners alike. Recordings, like paintings or sculptures, are frozen for ever: apparent variations in them can be experienced only by changes in the minds of the listener or the viewer.

11.2 Spontaneous performance

The aim of this chapter is not to teach formal extemporization or figured bass, jazz improvisation or the techniques of aleatoric music. Rather, it is concerned with the benefits which we can gain from bypassing the written page and focusing all our attention on the *sound* of performance and of composition.

As performers, the experience of improvising, of discovering that control of instrument or voice need not depend on having a printed page to rely upon, often increases our self-confidence. It can also greatly enhance our awareness of what is going on in an ensemble, as the second exercise in section 11.3 will make clear.

Many composers already stimulate their imaginations by improvisation. Some of it begins as keyboard 'doodling' which can be a valuable creative spur. Too often, musicians experimenting in this way are told to stop 'messing around' or to 'practise properly'. Many potential composers must have been thwarted by such mindless prohibitions! In fact, for some composers it is essential to experiment directly with sound, to

131

improvise, and only come to notating it later simply as a means of storing it and communicating it to others.

Strangely, many musicians become progressively less confident at doing anything away from a notated score. While all children begin to sing and play by ear, and will invent their own musical sounds quite spontaneously, the development of reading skills often inhibits improvising. The National Curriculum wisely requires pupils to improvise at every Key Stage. This musical freedom is too often lost when the assessment of 'right/wrong' drives the GCSE and 'A' level curricula.

11.3 Exercises and discussion

First, every instrumentalist chooses one note and experiments with it. (The only self-imposed constraint at this stage might be to limit the dynamic levels to avoid an unbearable cacophony of simultaneous improvisers!) Continue until this improvisation has been more-or-less memorized—although this, by definition, takes it a stage further towards considered composition. Next select two or three performers to demonstrate their improvisations in turn. Discuss each of them, in threes and as a group. Note down your conclusions. Do *not* read on until you have done this . . .

. . . to avoid being led by the following:

Possible comments may relate to how the one-note improvisation was structured. Did it have a shape, a sense of forward propulsion, of purpose? Was there any doubt about when it had ended? If not, it *must* have had some communicable structure, even if you cannot define it. Consider, too, how far the improvisation used the expressive elements. Were there variations of dynamics, of articulation, of timbre, of placing (did the performer stand still or walk about)? How far did it use actively changing sound, static sound such as the sustaining of a long note or a recurring rhythmic cell, or silence?

For the second exercise, select two performers, who should sit with their backs to each other. Agree a constraint such as limiting their improvisation to only two notes each—but the choice of those two notes is theirs. With no further constraints at all, no suggested form such as ABA, no suggested time limit, and no opportunity to discuss what they intend to do, invite them to improvise together. If the exercise is undertaken sincerely and seriously, remarkable things can result from it:

1. Almost certainly the piece will have a positive and unequivocal ending.
2. Very intense levels of listening arise where players are back-to-back and so there is no visual contact between them.
3. Recognizable structures arise too. Rhythms and intervals are imitated or reversed, dynamics rise to climaxes and fall away with unspoken unanimity.

The audience should identify and discuss what structural patterns appeared.

For the third exercise, repeat the second one with a new pair of performers but, this time, suggest some constraints within which to work: improvisation does not necessarily imply total freedom. For example, the performers might be invited to use only three notes, to create over two minutes an outline ABA form, and to keep within one dynamic level, pianissimo. Subsequent discussion cannot be predicted here, of course, but it should include some assessment of whether the piece made any kind of musical sense or had any coherence. If so, why? If not, why not? Repeat this exercise several times and over a period. If you can record the results, you are very likely to find that the whole process becomes more sophisticated, more imaginative and more intense as it becomes less of a novelty and instead a route to mutual relationships and co-operative creativity in music.

Finally, increase to three the number of people improvising together. First, play facing each other, and then facing outwards so that the only contact is by ear. The complexity of the musical interactions increases greatly with the addition of just one more person than the duo of the previous exercise. Listeners should continue to discuss the performances and comment on them. In particular, point out any ways in which the improvisations display structural organization, even though no plan has been made in advance.

11.4 Deepening awareness through improvisation

Most improvisation is within some set of constraints such as the context, for a concerto cadenza, of the mood, the style, the earlier melodic and rhythmic material of the movement. A consequence of this is that improvisation often expands and extends elements; in a concerto cadenza, it often serves as a final opportunity for development. The process of 'development' is one of discovering and then exposing the hidden potential of a musical idea. So, in classical sonata form, the recapitulation is not merely a return to the opening musical concepts; by now, our perceptions of them have changed and we comprehend them in the light of what has happened since their exposition. An analogous process happens in any art form needing time for its presentation. Our perception of characters introduced at the beginning of a novel or a play is quite different from our knowledge of them after we have observed their actions and reactions as the plot unfolds, even though the time-scale of this 'development' may be different from that experienced in music.

We can similarly deepen our knowledge of music by subjecting it to a process of development through improvisation. A composer does this as a matter of course: it is essential to composing music which holds together cogently. The process may take place in the head if the composer's memory can retain the burgeoning ideas—as could Mozart. Others fill notebooks with developmental possibilities: Beethoven is the outstanding example. But this process is invaluable for performers, too. It is a way of uncovering the potential, initially locked within a piece of notated music.

11.5 Exercise and discussion

Consider the opening bar or two of whatever piece you are currently learning to play. Examine the fragment carefully, noting which musical elements are employed in it. Perhaps it has a particular rhythmic feature, or stresses one or two intervals; perhaps a long note invites vibrato or a crescendo; or it may contain one or more characteristic textures or densities, span a notably wide or narrow range, call for a particular tone quality. When you have identified some of the elements which characterize it, improvise upon them. This may involve using the manipulatory devices described in section 8.2—*repeat* a feature, *sustain* it beyond its original durations, *reverse* it (piano instead of forte, arco instead of pizzicato), or *expand* it by exaggeration, on a string instrument taking sul ponticello right over the bridge on to the tail-piece end of the strings or, on a clarinet, flexing the embouchure until the sound breaks down altogether.

Discussion among the audience may produce proposals for extending the scope of this 'development' even further, or comments on whether the elements that have been distilled from the musical source really existed in embryo within it. Certainly, by the end of the exercise, the performer should have a much deeper understanding of the emotional and technical potential of the fragment, an understanding which can then enhance subsequent study, practice and, ultimately, performance.

11.6 Exercises and discussion

So far, the greatest number improvising together has been three. The complexity of the musical interactions seems to increase exponentially as this number is increased. Structural matters multiply too. So, to keep the complexity under control, a group of a dozen or so players may well find that they instinctively divide into subgroups, on the basis of instrumental families for instance.

First, improvise, with *no* preliminary discussion at all to determine any constraints or formal plan, in a group of any number from, say, six to fifteen. After this experience of *spontaneous* improvisation (which, by definition, can happen only once with a given piece), discuss it. Note particularly ways in which it benefited from its spontaneity—perhaps creating an entirely unpredicted sound of great beauty—and ways in which it suffered from the lack of any constraints and planning: perhaps rambling on indecisively, with no one taking the initiative to end it.

Second, engage in a planned improvisation, allowing ideas to be discussed and practised. So far, *form* has been largely arrived at fortuitously. In 11.2, your audience might have suggested improvising within ABA form, but the details, in 11.5 for instance, have been concerned with *structure*. (Chapter 8.1 will remind you of the difference between 'form' and 'structure', at least for the purposes of this book, though dictionary definitions tend to blur the important distinction.)

A planned improvisation can imply a predetermined form, many examples of which you will possibly have met and used before. The National Curriculum refers to 'beginning, middle, end' and 'repetition' within the first Key Stage. Later examples include such preformed moulds as ostinato, rondo and variations.

It goes without saying that the end result of playing to a pre-determined formal plan will not be totally extempore, any more than a wise concerto soloist or jazz instrumentalist will launch into a cadenza or a 'break' without some preparation. Discussion should highlight the difference between this *controlled* improvisation and the *spontaneous* experience of the first exercise.

Finally, most group activities throw to the fore a leader, a dominant character who takes decisions on behalf of the rest of the group. This often admirable quality, without which many performances might flounder in indecisive compromise, can be shared among several people in an improvising group as follows:

1. Take a short piece of music which one of your group can play. Almost anything will do provided either that it is known to all or it can quickly be made familiar by a few repeated playings.
2. Create a set of 'controlled improvisations' upon it, each lasting about 30 seconds and each led by a different person who may or may not choose to consult the others about what elements from the given piece are to be developed by improvisation, and how this is to be done.
3. Perform the improvisations, beginning and ending with the original piece, creating a set of variations framed by their source.

11.7 Recording

The performances which conclude all these exercises should be recorded, played back and discussed if at all possible. First, this provides a record with which to resolve argument about what actually took place, which avoids frustration during constructive discussion. Second, performers who are wrapped up in the process of improvisation find it a revealing experience to listen to it more objectively later. Finally, some of the musical results arrived at in this aleatoric fashion may be too engaging, too beautiful, for their creators to lose for ever.

11.8 Do-it-yourself exercises

First, improvise every day for a few minutes before beginning your practice. Let your imagination wander freely in search of new ideas and new constraints within which to develop them.

Second, record your improvisations and listen to them at leisure. Using the guidelines in Chapter 7, criticize them.

Finally, consider, and jot down a summary of, any improvisatory qualities you notice in a performance, live, broadcast or recorded. These will range from the detailed interpretative freedom allowed to performers playing fully composed music such as the ornamentation of a baroque vocal or instrumental line or the musical invention of live jazz, to the almost total freedom which may be given to a performer of contemporary aleatoric music.

12

Playing from memory

12.1 Removing barriers

One of the benefits of improvising (Chapter 11) is that it frees us from the written score. Instead of peering at symbols on a page, all our attention can be on the musical sound we are creating. In some situations, eyes can encourage ears to listen—following a score during the performance of a record can stop our minds wandering away from the music, seeing performers moving, watching the 'body language' of members of a chamber ensemble reacting to one another or an orchestra responding to a conductor, all can keep our ears focused on the sounds they are making. But in other circumstances, seeing can fog listening. Try an experiment: fix your eyes on something near you—the dial of your watch, say—and concentrate hard on it. Do so *now*, before reading on . . .

. . . Were you less aware than usual of the soundscape around you? This is the converse of the experiment in section 2.1 when your attention was focused wholly on listening, with your eyes closed. When reading music, the visual stimuli are all too likely to block our aural concentration. Sight-reading is the most extreme visually-centred activity. Experiment again by sight-reading four bars or so of anything, and then consider how much you actually *heard* apart from the crude pitches.

To a significant extent, looking at the music is a matter of habit. Nervous, inexperienced performers often take refuge behind the pages to an extraordinary degree. Next time you are at an amateur concert, see how many performers glare even at the very last chord of a piece, after they have played it and the notation has nothing more to offer. You may even do so yourself.

12.2 Focusing on sound alone

The aim of this chapter is to provide some experience of the deeper perceptions with which we can listen when our attention is not distracted by the sight of musical notation and all our concentration is on listening. Coupled with this experience are some suggestions about how to set about teaching yourself to perform from memory.

12.3 Aural memory

Although every one of us has to work out our own ways of memorizing, there are some well-tried aids to achieving it, and any group of musicians will have ideas to share with each other.

Share, in groups of three, any means you may have found helpful for memorizing securely. Then pool your ideas in a larger discussion (if you are working in a class). Alternatively, write a list of such ideas before reading on.

Many of those who have analysed memorizing identify four main ways in which to achieve it. One is through *aural* memory: if you can remember music in your head and are also adept at playing 'by ear' (the skill examined in Chapter 10), the two combine in playing from memory. This is very common with singers, so common in fact that they are *expected* to perform from memory except in oratorio (a strange and inexplicable convention) or in some particularly taxing recent music. Singers, of course, have a lifelong experience of close contact between the 'instrument' (the voice) and the brain. Similarly, children taught the violin from pre-school age and largely by imitation (as in the Suzuki method) are good at playing by ear. For them, once the *sound* of the music is memorized, there are few remaining problems in reproducing it, given the technical facility to do so. In musical cultures other than the western tradition, too, music is often learnt by observation and imitation, so that the finished performance is inevitably from memory: players of the Indian classical sitar and tabla do not sit with music stands in front of them.

Prove the value of this aural route to memorizing by playing any melody of which you have not previously seen a notated score. A pop song, a folk tune, a fragment of anything you might sing in the bath will do. The mere fact that we can all do this, accurately or with some stumbling, shows that aural memory, the recollection simply of how some music 'goes' coupled with playing by ear, is a constituent of playing from memory. It is really self-evident—but we need to be aware of it.

12.4 Visual memory

Visual memory can also be helpful. There are two options: to memorize the sight of the musical score, page by page, with a kind of photographic memory, and to memorize the sight of the part of the instrument upon which fingers move. This second kind of visual memory is widely used by guitarists, who often concentrate so hard on watching their left-hand fingers creating patterns on the finger-board that they are very poor sight-readers indeed. Some simply cannot play with eyes focused on notation, and have to learn by looking quickly up and down, from notation to fingers and back again. Pianists, too, often watch their own finger movements and can sometimes lose their place in the written music on the stand in front of them.

Players of bowed strings use this kind of visual memorizing less than keyboard players, while it is even less used by wind instrumentalists, and is physically impossible for bassoonists. But all can use visual memory of the written score to some extent, while a few claim to have a reliable and accurate photographic memory, capable of total recall of notation, sometimes retained over long periods of time.

Exercise and discussion

Give yourself the experience of one or both kinds of visual memory. Look for some moments at a bar or two of music unknown to you, for your own instrument. If you are working in a group and have nothing available—the next movement of the sonata you are learning or another piece in an anthology of graded pieces—get your neighbour to write a couple of bars for you. Try to fix the music visually in your mind; then play it. Next discuss, in groups of three, what helped you to succeed, or what caused failure.

Such discussion may hit upon the value of identifying patterns in the music—a sequence is easier to visualize than a random series of notes; fingerings can be as memorable as pitches; all the musical 'elements' (Chapter 2) in addition to pitch and rhythm need visualizing too, and may well help the 'mental eye' to recall the written page accurately.

Next, memorize visually the sight of hands in relation to keys, fingerboards or slides, if your instrument allows this. Again, learn a few seconds of music this way and then play it to your neighbour with eyes glued to the finger movements. Some pianists, in particular, find this a very valuable aid to memorizing or merely another trick to use when practising an awkward corner of a piece even if it is not finally to be totally memorized.

A disadvantage of visual memory is, of course, that the imaginary 'sight' of the printed music or the hands on the instrument still acts as a barrier to the deepest level of *listening*. If in section 12.1 you had merely thought of the sight of your watch dial rather than actually looking at it, your aural attention would still have been distracted.

12.5 Kinaesthetic memory

Kinaesthetic memory refers to recalling the sensation of muscular movement which we acquire after practising the same passage again and again. It is invaluable for certain conventional musical patterns such as scales and arpeggios, which constantly recur in western tonal music. So all of us, on seeing and identifying, say, an octave rising scale of C major in a piece, simply switch on the kinaesthetic memory of that scale which we have all practised innumerable times since we first began having instrumental lessons. We have no need to concern ourselves with

141

the notes between one C and the next an octave higher. The muscular movements are quite automatic, and the brain is free to think about other things—the tone-quality and dynamics of the scale, or the accompanying parts, or the phrase which follows the scale.

Kinaesthetic memory is invaluable in certain rhythmic situations too, such as playing 'two-against-three'. This can completely defeat the beginning keyboard player, or else can sound as stilted and artificial as the mnemonics which teachers invent to assist it, such as Ex. 12.5a.

Ex. 12.5a

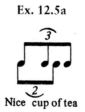

Nice cup of tea

Yet it can suddenly fall into place as kinaesthetic memory takes over one of the rhythms and the conscious brain is freed to think only of the other one.

Much as we use kinaesthetic memory in conventional patterns which we commonly learn in the course of our training—major, minor and chromatic scales, arpeggiated major and minor chords, dominant and diminished sevenths and so on—this approach to memorizing is very risky indeed. Miss one note of a passage of semiquavers, and all the following notes may be wrong; learn two similar patterns kinaesthetically and they are all too easily interchanged. It is not uncommon in the stress of public performance to get into an inescapable cycle where kinaesthetic memory takes the fingers back to an earlier part of a movement again and again so that both performer and audience wonder if there is any escape other than the embarrassment of total breakdown.

So, while kinaesthetic memory is invaluable for acquiring a sound repertoire of common musical patterns, it should be used very cautiously within the context of learning a specific piece. Hours of mindless repetition—the mind detached from the sensations of muscular movement—may create a superficial slickness but is a recipe for unpredictable disaster if it is not supported by other ways of memorizing.

12.6 Analytical memory

The fourth way of learning by heart is through analysis. You will have touched on this in the exercise in visual analysis in section 12.4—a sequence or a two-octave scale are virtually impossible to *visualize* without us also *rationalizing* the sequential pattern or the row of fifteen adjacent diatonic notes.

Exercise and discussion

Mental analysis culminating in memory can be done away from your instrument. Play Ex. 12.6a twice, from a recording, or on the oboe if an oboist is available, or on any other instrument.

Ex. 12.6a 'Bacchus', No. 4 from *Six Metamorphoses after Ovid*, Benjamin Britten (1913–76)

Then, with the sound now reasonably familiar to you so that this is not a basic 'imaging' exercise, analyse it silently for about four or five minutes before attempting to write it out from memory.

Finally, compare your copy with that of a couple of your fellow students and discuss how and why you may have achieved various levels of accuracy. Perhaps you wrote the pitches and note-values accurately having analysed the patterns: a first bar of

143

a repeated rising dotted-quaver-semiquaver and three rising semiquavers; a second bar of the inversion of the two-note figure twice, from B♭, and once higher, from C, before the semiquavers.

But what of the speed (crotchet = 112) and the clues to inter-pretation ('Allegro pesante', the '*f*'s, the slurs and staccatissimo articulatory marks)? By now, their importance should be clear—much of this book has been concerned with these elements of musical expression, so easily neglected in our concern for pitch and rhythm. But if some of these expressive elements were miss-ing, look again analytically at Ex. 12.6a for a while, and then amend your copy from memory.

12.7 Do-it-yourself exercises

First, consider the opening sixteen bars or so of a piece of music which you have learnt thoroughly, such as a piece prepared for an examination or played at a recent concert. Draw bar-lines and, within them, write down only the *dynamics* of these bars. (If you are unable to do so, sit with the piece away from your instrument and think about the dynamics—what they are, where they are, why they are patterned as they are. Then go back to the exercise.) Add phrasing and articulation markings to the skele-ton score. (Again, analyse them silently with the score if you can-not immediately do this from memory.) Add some kind of graphic indication of the timbral quality you seek in the piece, depending on where its tessitura lies within the compass of the instrument.

Next add metronome marking, tempo instruction ('allegro', 'grave', etc.), indications of flexibility in tempo as you interpret it (such as → and ← to indicate moving on and holding back within a phrase), and indications (not exact notation) of the piano accompaniment to a single-line instrument or the left-hand accompaniment to a piano right-hand melody—or what-ever is relevant to complete the texture of the piece you have chosen.

Then write out as much of the pitch and rhythmic notation as you can, in effect writing from your own mental 'dictation' a complete score of the piece, but *beginning* with those elements, of phrasing, dynamics, interpretational nuances, timbre and texture which are normally added as an afterthought to the pitches and rhythms of melodies and accompaniments. Finally, play the sixteen-or-so bars, preferably from memory, and assess whether your awareness of their subtleties has been sharpened by the exercise.

A second, invaluable exercise, which works only for keyboard players, is to take a few bars of a constant semiquaver figuration such as might occur in a classical sonata movement. Ex. 12.7a would serve the purpose.

Analyse its patterns and memorize the sounds *without* developing any kinaesthetic (muscular) memory by playing it many times, thoughtfully, with *only one finger*. When this becomes tedious, play it with the left hand. Use any means your intellect and aural memory can produce to retain it. Then attempt to play it, from memory, as the composer (Mozart) intended.

Whether or not this (difficult) exercise is immediately successful, one-finger or wrong-hand practice is a valuable means of penetrating deeply into a passage of music without developing the kind of dependence on muscular memory which so easily fails us when our minds are distracted by the tensions of public performance. Indeed, such deep mental analysis helps to keep the mind concentrating at such moments.

Finally, a revealing experience, once a piece of music is thoroughly memorized, is to play it in the dark. All visual distractions except a mental picture of the score are put aside; nothing impinges on the senses other than sound and touch.

12.8 From memory—with confidence

There is no intention in this chapter of insisting on memorized public performance for anyone who feels uneasy without the safeguard of the printed music. Fashions and conventions make quite irrational demands on us; pianists are expected to play from memory while organists are not. Yet, if a piece has been studied deeply enough to be performed responsibly to an audience, it should ideally have reached the point at which it *could* be played from memory. So the score can be used only as an *aide*

Ex. 12.7a Concerto in A major, K488, first movement, bars 86–98, W. A. Mozart (1756–91)

memoire, on a music stand placed to one side rather than as a barrier between player and audience, or laid flat on a grand piano rather than glared at, a visual distraction in the way of deep aural awareness.

Probably no one method, aural, visual, kinaesthetic or analytical, will work in isolation. Instead, each will combine or alternate with the others to focus attention not on the written notation but on the sounds which it symbolizes.

Postscript   Towards a deeper awareness . . .

The ideas contained within each chapter of this book have had to be expressed in some kind of order. Yet each is dependent on the others: memorizing and improvisation (Chapters 12 and 11) involve playing by ear (Chapter 10). The elements of musical expression (Chapter 2) can be revealed only within a coherent structure (Chapter 8). So it is worth reading quickly through the chapters again, considering now the early ones in the light of those towards the end.

The exercises are no more than a series of suggestions. Some will appeal to you, others will seem irrelevant depending on your particular musical needs—the techniques you use to compose, the instrument you play, and your tastes and ambitions as a listener. Some will be immediately suitable for group use at any level from primary school to conservatoire or university. Some are clearly open to development by making them longer or more demanding, working them with a higher level of performing technique. Many can be simplified, for use by class teachers in school or by instrumental or vocal teachers. Reduce length, limit perceptual expectations, simplify language.

So identify whatever exercises have proved useful to you and continue to use them indefinitely, adapting and developing them as your needs and skills develop. The aim has been to introduce a repertoire of ideas, not a series of inflexible routines. They are meant to emphasize matters neglected in other schemes of aural training, but to complement such schemes rather than provide a substitute for them. Many of them have themselves changed radically over recent years. Together with the other two identifiable musical activities, performing and composing, attentive and critical awareness is an essential ingredient of the National Curriculum in Music, termed there 'Listening and Appraising' and engaged in from the age of 5 upwards. The Associated Board of the Royal Schools of Music has revised the aural tests associated with its grade examinations to require musical judgement rather than solely factual information. Beyond the ABRSM's final Grade 8 level, the LRSM has an enlightened syllabus of 'Aural Awareness' and the CT ABRSM includes aural teaching, improvisation, listening and memorizing among its subject headings. For both of these courses, this book is a recommended text.

It is also the starting point for the CALMA Computer Assisted Learning package described in the Introduction, and available from early in the new millennium.

Aural awareness undergoes constant growth through a lifetime of musical activity. If this book aids that growth, it has achieved its purpose.

Appendix 1   Assessment

As conventional aural training programmes suffer from being driven by the need for assessment, so this alternative approach presents the opposite dilemma—that much of it is simply unassessable. Alas! This remains an issue in educational systems where achievement is often recognized only if it can be measured.

In an ideal world the rewards for concentrated study in aural perception should be in the enhanced control of a performer's technique, in the flair and precision of a composer's imagination, in the level of emotional and intellectual response enjoyed by a listener.

If this is not enough, the following assessment scheme creates targets for achievement without the kind of competitiveness which leads some very capable musicians to believe that they are 'bad at aural'. The scheme assumes that the book is used as the basic structure for a one-year course at undergraduate or sixth-form level. Other models can easily be devised for use in schools, or by private instrumental/vocal teachers.

Assessment 1 (30 per cent)—to follow Chapter 3, 'Aural synthesis'

Drawing on the initial study of musical elements, write a critique of, say, 600 words (about two sides of paper) of any one of three or four pieces of unfamiliar music selected by a tutor from available live performances or, failing that, recordings. If recordings have to be used, you must listen to them only once, to match the situation of a live performance. There is no requirement for profound judgements or deep emotional insight. Marks can be awarded for

1. the level of aural observation of musical elements;
2. the degree of understanding about how the elements interact to produce an effect;
3. the coherence of argument in this critical evaluation.

Assessment 2 (30 per cent)—to follow Chapter 6, 'Timbre'

Working in groups of three or four, students present projects in which each team undertakes to talk through a short passage of music, illustrating matters of articulation, register, timbre, etc. A possible strategy would be to make a comparison of different recordings of the same piece such as part of a *Brandenburg Concerto* movement played by a large romantic orchestra and by a baroque ensemble using authentic instruments. Marks can be awarded for

1. the effort put into, and the professionalism of, the class presentation;
2. the same qualities in the submitted written version;
3. the level of observation and the clarity of argument found in both.

Assessment 3 (20 per cent)—to follow Chapter 11, 'Improvisation'

Drawing on the ideas discussed and used in Chapter 8, 'Structure', and Chapter 10, 'Playing by ear', and working in groups of about six, students perform a group improvisation which has been prepared over two or three weeks. Each should last roughly five minutes and be followed by a brief description of how the group set about the task. A certain amount of notation is acceptable as an *aide memoire* and groups can even nominate a conductor or director if required. Written preparation should not, though, approach a conventional score and set of parts. Any style is acceptable other than extended pastiche, and marks can be awarded for

1. the coherence of large-scale structures;
2. the effectiveness of short-term interactions between players and the musical material they are controlling;
3. students' awareness of all the musical elements, particularly timbre, tessitura and the placing of sound in space.

The remaining 20 per cent of marks in this assessment scheme is for an informal log of experiences and progress which students should keep, in a folder, throughout the year. It will include any written 'Do-it-yourself' exercises, notes which may be taken from the explanatory sections of each chapter of this book and from any expansions of them offered by tutors, collections of concert programmes which may be annotated—in short, any evidence a student cares to show of inquiry, discovery and developing aural discrimination. Marks can be awarded largely on quantity, enthusiasm and readiness to experiment.

Appendix 2   Resources

There is no need for a large number of specific recordings to illustrate points made in this book. CD reference numbers are given in square brackets, [ ], simply as suggestions, perhaps to pass on to a school or university librarian as desirable acquisitions. In many cases, an illustration is suggested as a 'for instance', and one Haydn symphonic allegro, one minimalist piece or one pop group will serve as well as another to generate observations. In a few cases, however, a specific work is used as the basis for detailed discussion. Most are readily available and likely to remain so in future new recordings on CDs or in any new formats which may be developed. If any are unobtainable, tutors may care to adapt the exercises upon which they are based to alternative music. The suggested versions of recordings are:

Chapter 3

Mozart: Symphony No. 39 in E♭ (K543)
There are many recordings available. Two contrasting CD performances are suggested in 3.3. A further contrasting pair are the English Baroque Soloists, conducted by John Eliot Gardiner [PHIL 442 604-2] and the Berlin Philharmonic Orchestra, conducted by Herbert von Karajan [DG 429 668-2].

Appendix 2: Resources

Penderecki: Threnody for the Victims of Hiroshima
Polish Radio and TV Symphony Orchestra conducted by
S. Kawalla [CONI CDCF 168].

Chapter 8

Mozart: Quintet for Clarinet and Strings in A (K581)
There are many recordings available. In addition to Thea King
playing on a basset clarinet [Hyperion CDA66199], two other
interesting options are Gervase de Peyer with the Amadeus
Quartet [DG 437 646-2] and Benny Goodman with the
Budapest Quartet, recorded in 1938 [BIDD LAB140].
Ligeti: Lontano
Wergo WER 60163-50 and DC 439 808-2.

Chapter 9

Britten: Serenade for Tenor, Horn and Strings, Op. 31
There are several recordings. Britten himself conducts Pears,
Tuckwell and the London Symphony Orchestra on PEAR
GEMMCD9177 and (the same performance) DECC 425 996-
2.

Printed in the United Kingdom
by Lightning Source UK Ltd.
106307UKS00001B/67-69